GOD'S WARRIORS

Dramatic Adventures of
Rabbis in Uniform

GOD'S WARRIORS

Dramatic Adventures of Rabbis in Uniform

By

DOV PERETZ ELKINS

Rabbi, Temple Beth El
Rochester, N. Y.

Illustrations by
ISOBEL GOLDMAN

 JONATHAN DAVID PUBLISHERS
MIDDLE VILLAGE, N. Y. 11379

Library of Congress Catalogue Card No. 74-226
ISBN 0-8246-0168-8

Printed in the United States of America

TABLE OF CONTENTS

CONTENTS (*continued*)

In Loving Memory
of My Parents
EDWARD AND BERTHA
ELKINS

Acknowledgements

The writing of this book would have been impossible were it not for the help, advice and encouragement of many people.

Special thanks are extended to Rabbi Louis Barish, a distinguished scholar, devoted chaplain and good friend. Many of the ideas for the stories in this book were taken from the book he edited, *Rabbis in Uniform* (Jonathan David Publishers, 1962).

I am greatly indebted to the staff of the Commission on Jewish Chaplaincy of the National Jewish Welfare Board. My good friend and colleague, Rabbi David Max Eichhorn, recently retired from the Commission staff, read the entire manuscript and made several helpful suggestions. Mr. Bernard Postal, former Director of Public Information of the JWB, gleaned through his files to find interesting press releases which served as the basis for several of the stories. Mr. Postal also provided many of the photographs from the

Commission's files. In addition, he read the manuscript and made helpful comments. Rabbis Aryeh Lev and Elihu Michelson, also of the Commission staff, were helpful in the preparation of the book.

Appreciation is extended to Rabbi Bertram W. Korn, of Congregation Kneseth Israel of Elkins Park, Pa., whose historical studies on the Jewish chaplaincy during the Civil War and the Spanish-American War were very helpful. I am also grateful to all of the many chaplains and former chaplains who provided photographs of themselves.

Thank you also to my dear friend, Frank Brezel, whose literary abilities, critical editorial eye, and devotion to his chaplain were all exemplary.

I am very grateful to my devoted secretary, Pearl Ostroff, who typed the manuscript with meticulous attention to detail, and whose constant help enabled me to find time for this project.

Warm appreciation is extended to Chaplain (Major General) Francis L. Sampson, Chief of Chaplains of the U.S. Army, for his moving Preface.

I am especially pleased to acknowledge my indebtedness to Isobel Goldman, an old friend and now collaborator, for her beautiful illustrations which have greatly enhanced the appeal and attractiveness of this book.

The patience and encouragement of my beloved wife, Elaine, are always very precious to me.

Lastly, special recognition should be made to all of the brave and valiant warriors of God, the rabbis in uniform, living and dead, whose courage, valor, faith and devotion to God and America made these stories possible.

I am also delighted that my sons, Hillel and Jonathan, helped me by reading some of the stories and offering their evaluations.

DOV PERETZ ELKINS
Temple Beth El
Rochester, New York

Preface

Jewish chaplains have played an exciting and dramatic role in the Armed Forces of the United States, particularly during and subsequent to the Civil War. Wherever they have served, in peace or in conflict, they have carried the message of the Almighty to their Jewish brethren with unswerving devotion, and extended the comfort of their faith in times of stress.

As Chief of Chaplains, I deem it an honor that my rabbinical comrades will be honored by this scintillating relation of their service to mankind. And I have no doubt but that those who will read these stories will never forget the Warriors of God who consecrated their lives to His service.

Chaplain (Major General)
FRANCIS L. SAMPSON
Chief of Chaplains, U.S. Army

Introduction

CLERGY IN UNIFORM

The story of military chaplains goes as far back as the days of the Bible. In the Book of Deuteronomy, the Israelites are commanded as follows:

> When you come near to battle, the priest shall come forward and speak to the people, and say to them, 'Harken, O Israel, you draw nigh this day to fight against your enemies: Let not your heart faint; do not fear, or tremble, for the Lord your God goes with you, to fight for you against your enemies, to give you the victory.'

In the United States, Jewish chaplains were not officially accepted into the military until July, 1862, when Congress passed a law permitting ordained clergy of faiths other than Christianity to serve. How that law came about is the theme of the first story in this book.

The next military engagement in which our country was involved was the short Spanish-American War (April 12 to August 11, 1898). During those months two Jewish chaplains were given commissions, but neither of them was called to active duty. The only rabbi to be near the battle area was Rabbi Joseph Krauskopf. What he did and the contribution he made are described in Chapter II.

On April 9, 1917, only three days after the United States entered World War I, twenty-two national Jewish organizations joined together to form a body later known as the National Jewish Welfare Board (JWB). This organization was created for the purpose of recruiting and endorsing American rabbis into the military. To be accepted as a chaplain in the American Armed Forces, one has to be an ordained clergyman and must have the approval of some recognized national association of clergy. The JWB's Commission on Jewish Chaplaincy, made up of rabbis from all persuasions, must give its stamp of approval before the military will accept a rabbi into the service. This approval is called "endorsement." Since 1917, the JWB has endorsed hundreds of rabbis. The first group was endorsed to serve during World War I.

In October, 1917, Congress authorized six positions for military rabbis. The first ones to be endorsed and accepted were rabbis who had already signed up in the Armed Forces as enlisted men. Rabbi Elkan C. Voorsanger of St. Louis enlisted in the medical corps in April, 1917. By May, his hospital unit was in France, among the first 500 soldiers of the American Expeditionary Force in Europe. On November 24, Sergeant Voorsanger became Chaplain (First Lieutenant) Voorsanger. For gallantry under fire he received the Croix de Guerre and the Purple Heart Medal. He became the senior chaplain of the 77th Division, and supervised thirty other chaplains of all faiths.

When the United States entered World War I, in 1917, 149 rabbis volunteered to serve. Of these, thirty-four were accepted and endorsed by the JWB, and twenty-three received commissions. Many others served as civilians in groups like the Red Cross. Two civilian rabbis, Israel Friedlander and Bernard Canter, were murdered by Russian bandits in 1920 while on a war relief mission for the Joint Distribution Committee, a group devoted to helping war victims.

One rabbinical student, Michael Aaronsohn, served as an enlisted soldier, and was blinded during the Meuse-Argonne battle in September, 1918. Despite his handicap, he continued his rabbinical studies after the War, and was ordained in 1923.

One of the outstanding rabbis who served during World War I was Rabbi Lee J. Levinger. His exciting story is told in Chapter IV.

When Japanese bombs fell on Pearl Harbor in December 1941, there were twenty-four Jewish chaplains in the American Armed Forces. Half of all eligible rabbis in the United States offered their services during the second World War. Over 300 served; two were killed in action; two were wounded. Forty-six were decorated for bravery.

The earliest report of a chaplain helping the displaced victims of Hitler's madness came in March, 1943. Dozens of others performed miraculous, life-saving deeds for the welfare of those who escaped death in concentration camps. Several of these stories are told in this book, together with other tales of World War II chaplains.

During the war, the rabbis who served decided that when hostilities ended they would band together in a formal organization. On March 26, 1946, the Association of Jewish Chaplains was founded, comprised of all rabbis who were then serving or had served in the American military. Today, there are close to 1000 members.

When President Harry S. Truman sent American troops into Korea in June, 1950, there were only eighteen Jewish chaplains in all of the American Armed Forces. When hostilities ended in July, 1953, twenty-four had served in combat.

A few days after the Korean conflict erupted, the three major national associations of American rabbis took a step which was unprecedented in American history. Clergymen are exempt by law from military duty. The American rabbinate voluntarily gave up that exemption and imposed upon itself its own selective service system to be able to fill the quota of rabbis needed in the service.

Since 1950, the JWB, with the help of rabbinical seminaries, has assured the military authorities of an adequate supply of Jewish spiritual leaders. Scores of young rabbis have served from the time of the Korean conflict to the present. In serving both God and their country, their record has been a proud and exciting one.

The story of how a young rabbi serving in Vietnam arranged a Passover Seder, only a short time after his arrival, concludes this volume.

The stories contained herein are stories of faith, valor, and dedication. The author's profound hope is that all those who read them will be as inspired by them as he was. This will have been more than enough reward.

THE JEWISH CHAPLAIN WHO WENT DOWN WITH
THE S. S. DORCHESTER

THE JEWISH CHAPLAIN WHO SERVED UNDER "IKE"

CHAPLAIN LEVINGER (FOURTH FROM LEFT) WITH
WELFARE WORKERS IN FRANCE IN 1919

THE RABBI OF IWO JIMA

THE MAN WHO DARED TO SEE PRESIDENT LINCOLN

RABBI JOSEPH KRAUSKOPF ON TOUR IN CUBA

CHAPLAINS USING AMERICAN POWER BRING REFUGEES
TO PALESTINE

A CHAPLAIN PLAYS ARCHAELOGIST

DEATH ON ICY SEAS

BAR MITZVAH FOR 28 BOYS AT ONCE

THE BOY IN BED 16

CHAPLAIN DRYER AND HIS MIRACULOUS SEDER IN SAIGON

RELIGIOUS SERVICES CONDUCTED IN THE FIELD BY CHAPLAIN ELKINS

CHAPLAIN PREPARES YOUNGSTERS ON ARMY POST
FOR SUKKOT HOLIDAY

CHAPLAIN HASELKORN MEMORIAZING JEWISH DEAD IN FRENCH CEMETERY

THE FLYING AMERICAN RABBI

GOD'S WARRIORS
Dramatic Adventures of
Rabbis in Uniform

The Man Who Dared to See
President Lincoln

THE STORY OF THE FIRST JEWISH CHAPLAIN

"I want you to write directly to President Lincoln, Rabbi Fishel. He's the only one who can help us now." These were the words of Colonel Max Einstein, commanding officer of the 65th Regiment of the Fifth Pennsylvania Cavalry.

Rabbi Fishel had been refused an appointment as an officer in the U.S. Army.

This is how it happened.

In 1861, Colonel Einstein's men voted to have a man named Michael Allen serve as their chaplain, even though he was not an ordained rabbi. Michael Allen was a Hebrew teacher who knew how to conduct Jewish religious services.

However, he did not act as chaplain for very long. Someone complained that Allen's presence in the Army violated a law passed by the Congress in July of that year.

The law stated: "Every regimental commander will appoint a chaplain on the vote of the field officers and company commanders. The chaplain must be a regularly ordained minister of some Christian denomination."

Since Michael Allen was not a Christian, he could not serve as a chaplain in the Army.

After Allen gave in and resigned from the Army, Colonel Einstein and his regiment elected another chaplain, this time an ordained rabbi, Rabbi Arnold Fishel.

When Rabbi Fishel sent his request for appointment as an Army chaplain to the War Department, it was denied.

"We regret," began the letter to Rabbi Fishel from the War Department, "that we cannot appoint a member of your faith as a chaplain of the U.S. Army. The laws of Congress strictly direct that all chaplains be of the Christian religion."

The Jewish community all over the northern United States was in an uproar. Editors of Jewish newspapers and magazines wrote articles and editorials burning with insult.

"Are we second class citizens?" asked one editor. "How dare our government not permit us to have our rabbis serve as chaplains in the Army!"

Jewish leaders, including many rabbis, drew up petitions to Congress, demanding that the law be changed. Among the signers of the petitions were many Christians who thought it only fair and just for their Jewish countrymen to have spiritual advisors in the military.

After fighting for many weeks and months, an organization known as the American Israelites approached Rabbi Fishel with their advice.

"We agree with Colonel Einstein," they told him. "You must go to Washington and speak to President Lincoln himself. All of our petitions and protests have not helped. Only the President can help us get a Jewish chaplain."

"I think you are right, gentlemen," answered the rabbi. "I will see President Lincoln himself."

Prepared with letters of recommendation from the Board of Delegates of the American Israelites and from many groups of American political leaders, including one from the Republican Party of New York (President Lincoln's Party), Rabbi Fishel set out to see the President.

Many people tried to stop him. They told him that the matter was not important enough to take the time of such an important and busy man.

"Who are you," said some of Rabbi Fishel's friends, "to see the most important man in the United States about your personal problem?"

"This is not a *personal* problem," answered Rabbi Fishel. "This is America's problem. If Americans cannot respect the religious beliefs of all its citizens, then it is not living up to the high standards set by the founding fathers of our country, many of whom came here to find freedom to worship God as they pleased. Why shouldn't American Jewish soldiers be able to participate in services in the faith that *they* choose with an ordained minister of *their* religion?"

Despite all of the warnings, Rabbi Fishel listened to the advice of Colonel Einstein and the American Israelites.

Even those who advised him to go did not believe that he would ever be admitted.

On December 11, 1861, Rabbi Fishel went to the offices of the President, and told his secretary that he wanted to see him on urgent national business.

"My mission to President Lincoln," said the rabbi, "is of vital interest to the welfare of our great nation. Please urge him to see me just for a short time."

"I will ask him," said the President's secretary. "But he is very busy, and I am not sure if he has time in his schedule. Perhaps you can come back in a few weeks."

"No," replied Rabbi Fishel. "Please tell him that I would like to see him *today*!"

Rabbi Fishel sat in the waiting room outside the President's office for hours. Just as he was ready to get up and leave in despair, the secretary came over to him.

"Rabbi Fishel, the President will see you now."

The rabbi could not believe his ears. He jumped up and almost tripped as he approached the door of the President's office.

President Lincoln asked him to explain the nature of his visit.

"I come here, Mr. President, to insure the principle of religious liberty in our great nation. America is too important a country to let religious bigotry reign within its borders. I have been refused an appointment as a chaplain in the U.S. Army because I am Jewish."

President Lincoln sat at his large wooden desk. He listened carefully to the words of the rabbi. He very carefully read all of the letters handed to him by Rabbi Fishel.

Fishel sat anxiously awaiting the reaction of the President. "Will he throw me out? Will he have me jailed for daring to bring this matter to the busiest man in the nation?" he thought.

Finally, the President looked up from his desk and spoke.

"I think you are right, dear Reverend, sir. Something must be done. This is the first time this matter has come to my attention. I will look into it immediately. Thank you for your interest in the progress of our country. I wish all of our citizens were as interested in America as you are!"

A few days later Rabbi Fishel received a letter from the President.

My dear sir:

I find there are several particulars in which the present law in regard to chaplains is deficient. I now design presenting to a committee of Congress this information, and I shall try to have a new law broad enough to cover what is desired by you in behalf of the Israelites.

> Yours truly,
> A. LINCOLN

On March 12, 1862, the new law was passed by the Senate, and on July 17th by the House of Representatives. The President signed it immediately thereafter. It was finally legal for a rabbi to be appointed chaplain.

One hundred years later, in 1962, Jews all over America celebrated the centennial of the Jewish military chaplaincy with meetings and tributes to the Jewish chaplains who served in all of America's wars.

All of this was due to the persistence of one devoted American—Rabbi Arnold Fishel—who dared to see the President himself.

The First Jewish Chaplain in Combat

THE STORY OF RABBI FERDINAND SARNER

The honor of being the first rabbi to serve with his men in combat fell to a man who did not even come to the United States until age 39.

Rabbi Ferdinand Sarner was a scholarly man who received many degrees in Germany. In January, 1859, when he had finished his studies, he decided to come to America.

Rabbi Sarner had been in America for only four years when he decided to enlist in the Army at Brooks Station, Virginia. He did not speak English very well, and somehow it was not clearly understood that he was a rabbi and not a Protestant minister.

At the meeting of the officers of the 54th New York Volunteer Regiment on April 10, 1863, Rabbi Sarner presented his credentials.

"I would like to be your chaplain," said the rabbi to the soldiers. "Here is a letter to testify to my abilities."

One of the officers took the letter.

"This is from the Prussian Ambassador in Washington!" exclaimed the officer.

Other certificates and letters presented by Rabbi Sarner were from important leaders in Berlin and Hesse.

"Please step outside the room," they said to Rabbi Sarner. "We want to discuss this matter and vote on it."

Rabbi Sarner took his coat, and went next door for the duration of the meeting.

One of the officers began to discuss the qualifications of the prospective chaplain.

"He speaks fluent German," he began. "Since we have many German immigrants in the regiment, this will be of great help."

"His letters of recommendation all speak very highly of him," said another. "He seems like just the man we need. I'm all for him."

"What religious group does he represent?" asked one of the officers.

"I'm not sure, I couldn't understand what he said when I asked him," explained the head officer. "But I imagine that he's a Lutheran since he comes from Germany, and has a letter from the Prussian Ambassador in Washington."

"We all agree then," said a few of the others in chorus. "Let's vote."

The vote was taken, and Rabbi Ferdinand Sarner was, of all things, elected to be the Lutheran minister of the 54th New York Volunteer Regiment.

On April 10, 1863, he was officially presented with his Certificate of Commission as an Army chaplain. The certificate read, "We hereby certify that Ferdinand Sarner will serve as the Chaplain of the 54th New York Volunteer

Regiment. He is a regularly ordained minister of the Lutheran Church."

Rabbi Sarner was so proud to be elected chaplain that he did not even look carefully at the certificate. He saw his name written on it in bold letters, and that was enough for him.

Some days later, Sarner showed the certificate to a friend. He was more than a little shocked to learn what it really said. But, when he explained the truth to his commanding officer, he was accepted just the same. Even though only three of the thirteen officers were Jewish, and only a few of the enlisted men, Chaplain Sarner served well as chaplain of the entire regiment.

He served so well, in fact, that his exceptional bravery caused him to be wounded in action.

His regiment served in many places, such as Chancellorsville, Virginia, on May 2-4, 1863. During the Battle of Gettysburg (July 1-4, 1863), Chaplain Sarner followed his men right to the battlefield, as was his custom. Wherever the men were, that was where he was found.

In the midst of the battle, an enemy cannon hit the chaplain's horse and killed it. When the horse fell, the chaplain fell to the ground. He was wounded seriously in the leg and hip.

The Battle of Gettysburg was very bloody, and Chaplain Sarner lay there in great pain watching his fellow soldiers wounded and killed. His pain was greater because he could do nothing to help them. He tried to rise and go to comfort some of them, but it was of no use. His wound was so bad that he could not move an inch.

When the battle was over, he was taken to a military hospital with the other casualties. He recuperated there until the doctors felt he was well enough to go back into action.

Chaplain Sarner joined his regiment once again and fought with them in the invasion of South Carolina. But he never fully recovered from his wounds at the Battle of Gettysburg, and he continued to walk with a heavy limp.

In July, 1864, he had to return to the hospital. At that time, he received the sad news.

"I am afraid, dear Chaplain," said his physician, "that your leg will never heal properly. We will have to discharge you."

Chaplain Sarner was no expert in military matters. He did not understand that he would have to wait for official orders to leave the hospital. His discharge came through from the War Department in October, 1864, but he had already left.

Since he was not present to receive the papers, he was charged with being AWOL (absent without leave). For five years, the Army tried to get in touch with him, unsuccessfully. Finally, in 1869, his discharge orders were changed to read as follows:

"The order which honorably discharged Chaplain Ferdinand Sarner, 54th New York Volunteers, on account of physical disability, is hereby amended to discharge him for absence without leave."

Thus, Rabbi Sarner was the first Jewish Chaplain to serve in combat, and the first (and only) one to be charged as AWOL.

No one knew that he was so discharged, and under the circumstances it would not have made any difference. His heroism under fire was well known.

It is one of the strange facts of history that this heroic rabbi and soldier, who lived through war and battle wounds, died of yellow fever in 1878.

The War Without Chaplains

THE STRANGE EVENTS OF THE
SPANISH-AMERICAN WAR

When the United States declared war on Spain in April, 1898, the Jewish community was totally unprepared. Although some four thousand Jewish soldiers served in the half-year war, not one Jewish chaplain was officially commissioned during this time.

After the outbreak of World War I, a national committee was formed to recruit, service and advise rabbis in the American military. This committee became known as the National Jewish Welfare Board. Today, the JWB, as it is called, is looked upon as an indispensable organization in American Jewish life. Its lack of existence in 1898 was sorely felt.

It is true that there were four Jewish chaplains appointed

during the Civil War, but their commissions were granted only for the duration of hostilities. In 1898, there was not one Jewish chaplain in all of the American military.

It was not until July of that year that a national organization of rabbis wrote to President McKinley requesting that he appoint a rabbi to serve the Jewish men in service. But the effort was undertaken too late. By August, the war had ended.

There were, however, two rabbis who deserve special mention for their devoted service during this period of crisis.

Both of these rabbis were serving at Congregation Kneseth Israel of Philadelphia. The first was Rabbi J. Leonard Levy, Associate Rabbi of the congregation, who had been there since 1893. During this period of American history, there still remained informal, civilian "volunteer" military units, which had been very popular during the Civil War. Late in May, 1898, the rabbi received a letter from Charles M. Keegan, a young tobacco salesman who had organized a volunteer brigade, inviting him to become spiritual leader of "Keegan's Brigade of Pennsylvania Volunteers."

Rabbi Levy referred the matter to the Board of Directors of the synagogue, who promptly and unanimously voted on May 29, 1898 to permit Rabbi Levy to accept the position offered by Colonel Keegan. Furthermore, they agreed to pay him his full salary during his period of military service. The rabbi announced his acceptance, and declared that he would donate any salary received from the government "to the relief of all cases of distress occasioned in the families of men who go as volunteers."

The public was deeply moved by this patriotic gesture, and shortly thereafter other officers of the Brigade followed his example by making similar declarations.

The men of the Brigade were desperately hoping that the War Department would give them official recognition, and call them to active service. But at this time government policy began to frown upon such volunteer units whose self-appointed officers were without military experience.

When August rolled around, Rabbi Levy had still not been honored with wearing the uniform of his country, and the war was over. It was truly a disappointment to him, because he was a fierce patriot and a dedicated servant of Judaism and America. When the Spanish-American War had just begun, he said the following in his sermon from the pulpit of Keneseth Israel on the morning of April 24, 1898:

> "... I hope it may be my privilege to lend my support to my country in the hour of trial. I hope it will be my privilege to undertake some service compatible with my calling during the present difficulty ..."

Shortly thereafter, at a public rally, he said the following:

> "... when ... murdered men and outraged women and children look to this great nation for aid, shall we refuse their appeal? No, not if we are Americans, the children of the heroic Washington and lovers of the martyred Lincoln ..."

Although Rabbi Levy was never able to realize his dream to serve his country, his "senior rabbi" did. Rabbi Joseph Krauskopf, one of the pre-eminent clergymen of his time, was appointed to be Field Commissioner of the National Relief Commission. Although he did not serve as military chaplain, he toured military camps in Washington, D. C., Jacksonville, Fernandina and Tampa, Florida, Chickamauga and Atlanta, Tennessee, Montauk Point, Long Island, and Cuba. His job was to report on sanitary and medical conditions in the camps, and on the morale of the soldiers. His reports helped the government correct many unhappy situations.

Even though his primary mission was not to serve only Jewish men, he never forgot that he was a rabbi. He constantly sought out Jewish soldiers. He counseled them, conducted services, and brought back messages to their families.

He was able to distribute 1000 copies of the Jewish prayer-book, a gift from the Central Conference of American Rabbis.

In his diary, Rabbi Krauskopf describes the services he conducted on the ship sailing to Cuba:

Sunday, July 24, 1898

... Last evening, the captain of the vessel approached me and asked me to conduct the Sunday service. I hesitated at first but finally consented, and so at 10:30 crew and passengers assembled in the large marines' mess room, and I conducted the entire service ... Found four Jewish men among the crew. This is indeed history. A rabbi conducting services for a gentile audience in an auxiliary U.S. Cruiser, along the coast of Cuba, at the request of a gentile U.S. Commander. I claim the honor of having conducted the first Jewish service in Cuba, or in that part of it that has recently surrendered to the United States ... The Jewish boys have just asked me for paper and stamps to write home. I shall look after their interests ...

During his stay in Cuba, the rabbi toured all the fighting fronts on horseback, becoming filthy and hungry and exhausted along with all the rest of the men. Week after week he investigated villages, camps, warehouses and hospitals, sometimes with scarcely any rest, to see that American servicemen were provided the very best care. On one trip to Cuba he even met a member of his own congregation, serving in the Army. Imagine how they felt to see each other so far from home!

After he returned home, the rabbi kept contact with many of the people he met in Cuba, including Theodore Roosevelt, later President of the United States, who was then colonel of the famous "Rough Riders." Roosevelt became one of the devoted admirers of Rabbi Krauskopf.

And so, although no official Jewish chaplain served during the Spanish-American War, two rabbis from a Philadelphia synagogue did their best to serve their beloved country in a very grave hour in its history.

Postscript

The information supplied in this story was dug up from old newspapers and documents by a noted Jewish historian, Rabbi Bertram W. Korn, in his article in the June, 1952, issue of the *Publication of the American Jewish Historical Society*. Rabbi Korn is presently rabbi of the same congregation in Philadelphia (now in a suburb called Elkins Park) from which Rabbis Levy and Krauskopf hailed, Keneseth Israel. He is also one of the highest ranking chaplains in the U.S. Naval Reserve.

A Jewish Chaplain in France

CHAPLAIN LEE J. LEVINGER IN WORLD WAR I

Rabbi Lee J. Levinger was commissioned as a First Lieutenant on Independence Day, 1918, only four months before
the end of World War I. His entire tour of service was only
eleven months long, including nine months with the American Expeditionary Forces in Europe. His experiences were
so dramatic, however, that he wrote an entire book, *A Jewish
Chaplain in France*, to describe them.

To prepare himself for his new military position, Rabbi
Levinger spent a short time at the Chaplain Training School
in Camp Taylor, Kentucky. There he met a lanky, back-
woods preacher from the South, with whom he shared a
bunk. When the preacher kept delaying turning off the lights
one night, the rabbi asked what kept him awake.

"I don't want to go to bed till I see how a Jew says his

15

prayers," he replied in a southern drawl. Levinger sat up with his mouth wide open in surprise.

This was the first surprise of many that Rabbi Levinger encountered during his eleven months of service. In the Army he met many people, clergy and laymen, who had never seen a Jew before. Often he felt himself to be like a monkey in a cage. This feeling was to stay with him during his many travels.

One of his trips, in August, 1918, took him to Europe. After thirteen uneasy days on the ship Balmoral Castle, constantly on the lookout for an enemy submarine, he landed in France.

Upon arrival, he found himself to be the only Jewish chaplain in all of France. At his orientation meeting, together with thirty-five Christian chaplains, he was called upon to teach his non-Jewish colleagues how to lead a dying Jewish man in prayer. In turn, he was advised of the requirements of Catholic and Protestant men in their last moments. Chaplains had to be prepared to serve men of all faiths. Often, there was only one chaplain for men of five or six different creeds. So every chaplain had to be prepared to lead men of all religions in their own rites. To this day, all chaplains are taught the final before-death prayers for men of the major faiths.

Rabbi Levinger's first assignment was to conduct High Holy Day Services at Nevers, France, the headquarters of the Intermediate Section of the Supply Service.

Men were invited to attend this service from many parts of France, from as far away as 100 miles. Rabbi Levinger spoke to his commanding officer about getting Jewish men furloughs to attend the services in Nevers. The following orders were issued:

> Wherever it will not interfere with military operations, soldiers of Jewish Faith will be excused from all duty and where practicable granted passes to enable them to observe Jewish Holidays. . . .

Nevers was a historic town of 30,000 residents, on the banks of the River Loire. All its streets were alleys with narrow sidewalks. Its lovely parks and squares gave it a quaint touch, and made it a pleasant place for a holiday retreat.

Jewish soldiers thronged into Nevers with great enthusiasm. Some of them had walked up to ten miles to catch the train to Nevers. Every hotel in town was completely filled by the afternoon of September 6, 1918, the day of Rosh Hashana, the Jewish New Year. Many soldiers had to find rooms in the homes of local residents.

Although the services were held under great handicaps, it was a wonderful spiritual experience for the men. There was no Torah scroll to read from, no *shofar* (ram's horn) to blow, not even a complete prayer book. There wasn't even a synagogue large enough to accommodate the great numbers of Jewish soldiers. Instead, a large, bare room at the local Y.M.C.A. was used.

But all of these obstacles were overlooked, and Rabbi Levinger was thanked again and again by those attending, for the fine services and the inspiring message he left with them in the sermon.

On September 20, Chaplain Levinger left Nevers, with great sorrow in his heart. But he knew that there were other Jewish men in France, and since he was the only Jewish chaplain, he wanted to travel as quickly as he could to visit with as many Jewish men as possible. When the Jewish Welfare Board of the United States provided him with an automobile, it became much easier for him to travel from place to place.

Rabbi Levinger was surprised to see many non-Jewish soldiers who happened to be in the area during prayer hour at his services. At some services up to 80% of the congregation was composed of non-Jews.

At such times, some of the Jewish men asked the rabbi to lead the service entirely in English, completely omitting

Hebrew from the prayers. Rabbi Levinger was willing to cooperate, and in fact, once conducted an entirely English service.

At the end of the service many of the Christian men came up to the rabbi and asked him to please restore the Hebrew in the service next time. They told him how much they enjoyed the rituals of the skull cap, and prayer shawl (*talit*), and the mystical quality of the ancient Hebrew prayers. He complied with their request gladly.

At times of war all men feel as one, and the differences between them become vehicles of friendship, instead of walls to divide. Experiences like this gave Chaplain Levinger a warm feeling of great accomplishment, in helping all Americans to pray together and work together for a common cause: Peace.

Once when travelling through the French town of Lyons, Rabbi Levinger was told a story about the rabbi of the city, Rabbi Bloch, who had served as Jewish chaplain to the French Army. Rabbi Bloch was seen by some fellow soldiers holding a cross before a dying Catholic, helping him recite the Confession, when an enemy bullet ended the rabbi's own life.

At one service, the chaplain was calling off the list of the dead in the company. In the middle of reading the names, he heard a shout from the back of the room, "I'm not dead, Chaplain." The group broke out in hysterical laughter, to release their sorrow and tension. It seems that two comrades had seen him fall with a wound in the head, and assumed he was killed. Luckily, the wound was only minor and he had already returned to duty.

In November of 1918 the armistice was called, and the fighting ceased. A party was held for Lt. Robert Bernstein, who had predicted in advance that November 11th would be the last day of the war. But Rabbi Levinger was in no mood to celebrate. He had just learned that one of his twin babies had died of influenza. (This disease caused the death of thousands of Americans in 1918, while today it is cured almost as routinely as a common cold.) The baby had died a month before, but the chaplain was out of communication during that time. He experienced great personal sorrow, though it helped him understand the pain and grief of the many American parents who lost their sons in battle.

After the War, Rabbi Levinger remained in France for seven months. There was much work left to be done such as gathering the names of the Jewish boys who had died and notifying the families involved. He also saw to it that every Jewish grave was marked with a Shield of David, and that the exact location was noted for the parents of each martyred soldier.

One of the very pleasant experiences for Chaplain Levinger after the war was witnessing General Pershing review the troops and decorate 100 men at one ceremony, of whom six were his co-religionists.

Rabbi Levinger spent Passover, 1919, at Le Mars, where over 1000 soldiers attended the Passover Seder meal. Soon after, he received orders to return home on the Noordam, a Holland-American line ship.

His boat anchored briefly at Brest, a French port city where the chief naval station was located. When he arrived there, he was told that four young sailors had just accidentally drowned outside the harbor. In the absence of a Christian chaplain, he conducted the funeral.

There he was, at the end of his military tour of duty, a Jewish Army chaplain conducting a naval funeral for four Christian sailors!

After twelve days at sea, Lee J. Levinger arrived in the United States and on May 26, 1919 received his honorable discharge at Fort Dix, New Jersey. He left the service with memories that would cling to him for the rest of his life.

The Rabbi Who Wore a Christian Insignia

THE STORY OF THE
FIRST JEWISH NAVY CHAPLAIN

Only one rabbi served as a Navy chaplain during World War I. His name was David Goldberg.

One afternoon in the summer of 1917, Rabbi Goldberg received a telephone call from United States Senator Morris Sheppard of Texas.

"Hello, Rabbi Goldberg," said the senator. "How would you like to serve in the United States Navy, as the first chaplain of your faith?"

"I would be deeply honored," answered the rabbi. "But, where did you get my name?" he asked, bewildered.

"From a distinguished gentleman . . . the most prominent

rabbi in all of Texas . . . Rabbi Henry Cohen of Galveston."

"Rabbi Cohen recommended me?" said David Goldberg, flattered and surprised at once.

"You can start as soon as I put the papers through. Good luck, Rabbi."

Everyone admitted that the appointment of a rabbi to the Navy was a welcome step, but no one knew exactly what to do with him. Chaplain Frazier, the head of the Navy Chaplains Corps, thought it would be best for him to spend two weeks at each of the principal Navy Yards and Training Stations so that he could visit all the Jewish men in the Navy. However, his suggestion was overruled by Secretary of the Navy Daniels.

Daniels wrote the new chaplain that he was not to be a roving rabbi, but a Navy chaplain, and Navy chaplains had to have a tour of sea duty prior to promotion. This was the first disappointment for Rabbi Goldberg. Being assigned to the U.S.S. President Grant, he had to minister to the religious needs of 600 men, only five of whom were of his own faith.

The second disappointment was even greater. There was no Jewish chaplaincy insignia in the Navy at that time. In the Army, Christian chaplains wore the Christian cross, and Jewish chaplains wore the six-pointed star, the "Shield of David," or *Magen David*. When people went looking for the Jewish chaplain, and found a man named Goldberg wearing a cross, they could not believe their eyes.

"Are you Father Goldberg?" asked one young sailor.

"No, young man, I am *Rabbi* Goldberg."

"Then how is it you are wearing the cross?"

This conversation was repeated a hundred times, if once. After a while, Chaplain Goldberg began to tire of telling the story. He sat down to write a letter to the Bureau of Navigation. In the letter, he asked to substitute the six-cornered Shield of David for the cross.

The letter was dated May 10, 1918. On June 14, an

answer came. He could not wear the six-pointed star, but perhaps he could suggest a suitable substitute.

The idea came to Chaplain Goldberg that a shepherd's crook might be suitable. (A crook is a staff carried by the shepherd with a hook at one end to catch sheep by the hind leg.) Since all clergymen are pastors or "shepherds" who serve their flock, the shepherd's crook could be used for all chaplains.

In fact, the shepherd's crook was the first insignia of the U.S. Army Chaplaincy, first used after the Civil War. In 1898 the cross had taken it place.

Chaplain Frazier did not like the idea of having all chaplains wear the shepherd's crook. Being a Christian minister, he knew that Catholic and Protestant chaplains would not want to give up wearing the cross, the most important symbol of their religion.

"I would not mind, though," wrote Chaplain Frazier, "if you and any other future Jewish chaplains choose an insignia for yourselves other than the cross."

Finally, on July 26, 1918, Secretary of the Navy Daniels gave his official approval to the shepherd's crook as the Jewish insignia.

Eventually, the insignia for Jewish chaplains in all branches of the armed services of the United States became the two tablets of the ten commandments, with the six-pointed star on top of it. Today, when a young soldier or sailor sees the tablets and the star with six points, he knows he is looking at a Jewish chaplain. All Christian chaplains, both Catholic and Protestant, today wear the cross, the symbol of Christianity and the crucifixion of Jesus.

In the summer of 1919, Chaplain Goldberg saw that many reserve chaplains were returning to civilian life. After more than two years of service, he submitted his resignation. During those two years, he served Christian and Jew to the best of his ability.

Through his pioneering efforts, Jewish chaplains who followed him could wear the insignia of their own faith. The many rabbis who served in the Navy after Rabbi Goldberg were able to serve many more Jewish sailors than the first rabbi in the Navy. But they also continued to serve young Christian Americans, as Christian chaplains serve Jews.

Chaplain Goldberg's pioneering work will always be remembered in the annals of Navy history.

Death on the Icy Seas

THE STORY OF CHAPLAIN ALEXANDER D. GOODE

The signal officer of the S.S. Dorchester was standing on the ship deck casually staring out at the blue sea when an ensign called to him in an excited voice:

"Sir, the coast guard cutter is blinking an important announcement. Stand by while I receive it."

"O.K., Barnes, I'm waiting," replied the lieutenant.

The men on the ship began to feel a tension in the air when they heard this. There was a funny feeling that danger was brewing.

"Barnes, have you finished receiving the message?" shouted the signal officer to the sailor on the lookout tower.

"Yes, sir," he replied. "There is a German submarine following us."

A wave of fear spread through the ship. Young sailors

and soldiers on the ship, many only recently beginning their tours of duty with the armed services, began to yearn for the warmth and security of their homes.

Through all of the anxiety, the four chaplains on the ship tried to comfort the men.

"Don't let it worry you," said Father Washington, Roman Catholic chaplain aboard. "All we can do is try our best, and leave the rest to God."

Similar attempts to give the men courage and confidence were made by Chaplain George Fox and Chaplain Clark Poling, Protestant chaplains, and Chaplain Alexander Goode, Jewish chaplain.

On the morning of February 3, 1943, at the first moment of dawn, while many were sleeping in their bunks and others stood watch on deck, a sudden explosion ripped the boat almost in two. What the men feared had actually happened. The Germans torpedoed a direct hit from their submarine. Fire broke out on all sides. Explosions in the boiler room rocked the ship violently.

"Abandon Ship!" was heard above the cries of sailors scrambling to escape the flames and destruction. The sea water was invading the old freighter rapidly. It would only be a matter of minutes before it dipped its sides completely beneath the waters. A thousand men rushed to and fro, trying desperately to jump to safety into the icy waters.

Life rafts were lowered, and scores jumped on. Others donned their life belts and gloves and dove overboard.

Lt. John Mahoney was standing next to Chaplain Goode when he noticed that he had forgotten his gloves. "I must go back and get them," he muttered aloud.

"Don't bother," said the rabbi. "Take mine, I have an extra pair."

Lt. Mahoney escaped into the frozen sea. He waited eight hours until picked up by a crowded life boat. "Without the chaplain's gloves my fingers would have frozen stiff," he later reported. "I never would have made it. As it was, only two of us survived out of the forty who were in our lifeboat. I owe my life to those gloves."

Lt. Mahoney later found out, from another survivor, that the rabbi really did not have another pair of gloves. Nor did he have another life belt when he gave his to an enlisted man, telling him, too, that he had another.

The other three chaplains on the ship acted in the same manner, giving up their only chance of escape to a fellow soldier or sailor.

After a very short time the ship dropped to the bottom of the Atlantic, never to be seen again. At the last moment of life, people in the life boats saw the "Four Chaplains" standing together on the deck, arms locked, each man offering prayers in the tradition of his own religion. One prayed in Hebrew, another in Latin, the other two in English. Together they breathed their last breath as the chill of the sea became a blanket that snuffed out their lives, and the ocean became their grave.

Seven hundred men died on the S.S. Dorchester on that bleak, bitter February morning in 1943. Only 300 lived to tell the story of the Four Chaplains who died standing together in prayer, surrendering their lives so that others could live.

For his part in the heroic act of the four chaplains, Rabbi Alexandre D. Goode posthumously received the Purple Heart and the Distinguished Service Cross.

Eight years later, a chapel on the campus of Temple University in the heart of Philadelphia, was dedicated. It is known as The Chapel of the Four Chaplains. On the wall of the chapel is a mural, depicting the last moment of life of the famous Four Chaplains. At the front of the chapel are three revolving arks, one Protestant, one Roman Catholic, and one Jewish. Men of all faiths can conduct services there by merely turning the appropriate altar in the frontward direction. The chapel is used by groups of all faiths, and as they pray there they recall the dramatic story of the men of God who died for their brethren.

The Chapel of the Four Chaplains was dedicated on February 3, 1951, the eighth anniversary of the sinking of the S.S. Dorchester.

At the dedication ceremony, then President of the United States, Harry S. Truman, spoke.

> We must never forget that this country was founded by men who came to these shores to worship God as they pleased. Catholics, Jews and Protestants, all came here for this great purpose . . . The unity of our country is a unity under God. It is a unity of freedom, for the service of God is perfect freedom. If we remember our faith in God, if we live by it as our forefathers did, we need have no fear of the future.

Above the entrance to the chapel there is an eternal light. Near it, chiseled in stone, is the following word of caution to all who enter:

> Chapel of Four Chaplains
> An Interfaith Shrine
> Here is Sanctuary for Brotherhood
> Let it Never be Violated

The Rabbi of Iwo Jima

THE STORY BEHIND THE FAMOUS SERMON OF RABBI ROLAND B. GITTELSOHN

On May 30, 1945, Rabbi Roland B. Gittelsohn, Jewish chaplain with the Fifth Marine Division, delivered the most famous sermon of any chaplain who served in the Second World War.

The occasion was the dedication of a military cemetery on the island of Iwo Jima. The cemetery was made necessary by the many deaths that occurred during the bloody battles of the previous months. Hundreds and thousands of American GIs died for the freedom of America and for the honor of her name.

The invitation to give the sermon came from the Senior Division Chaplain, Warren F. Cuthriell.

"I want you to preach the sermon on Dedication Day,

Rabbi," said Chaplain Cuthriell, "because you are the chaplain for the smallest religious minority. These men died for the right to preserve America and her belief in freedom of religion, and I think that they would have liked it this way."

Chaplain Gittelsohn was deeply honored and he spent ten days etching a moving address out of paper and ink. His efforts were well worth it. His sermon became known throughout America, and many still know it as the most repeated sermon delivered during World War II.

Chaplain Gittelsohn, in his speech written for the combined religious dedication ceremony, paid loving tribute to these fighting men of all faiths.

In part, he said:

> This is perhaps the grimmest, and surely the holiest task we have faced since D-Day. Here, before us lie the bodies of comrades and friends. Men who, until yesterday or last week, laughed with us, joked with us and went over the sides with us as we prepared to hit the beaches of this island . . .
>
> Here lie officers and men, Negroes and whites, rich and poor, together. Here are Protestants, Catholics and Jews, together. Here no man prefers another because of his faith, or despises him because of his color . . . Among these men there is no discrimination, no prejudice, no hatred. Theirs is the highest and purest democracy. Any man among us, the living, who fails to understand that, will thereby betray those who here lie dead. Whoever of us lifts his hand in hate against a brother, or thinks himself superior to those who happen to be in the minority, makes of this ceremony and of the bloody sacrifice it commemorates, an empty, hollow mockery . . .

The great tragedy of this sermon is that it was never delivered at the interfaith service. In fact, no interfaith service was ever held!

Just a day before the dedication ceremony, after Chaplain Gittelsohn had already completed his sermon, a group of non-Jewish chaplains came to Chaplain Cuthriell and declared that they would not attend the service if it were conducted by a rabbi! Most of the men were Christian, they said, and a Christian must preside over the service.

Chaplain Cuthriell used all of his persuasive abilities trying to convince the Christian chaplains that their attitude wasn't fitting. Nothing helped.

With a sad heart, Chaplain Cuthriell called Chaplain Gittelsohn into his office and reported the news.

"I have decided," he said with a look of deep disappointment on his face, "that we will have to have separate services instead of one joint service. That is the only way in which all of the chaplains will participate."

Rabbi Gittelsohn walked out broken-hearted. "The men buried in this cemetery," he thought to himself, "died so that religious freedom could be the possession of Americans of all faiths, and so that Americans of every religion could walk proudly and unafraid, free of prejudice and hatred. This action is un-American."

And so, Rabbi Gittelsohn's sermon was not delivered as planned. It was not delivered at a joint interfaith service for all the marines on Iwo Jima, but at a small Jewish service which took place after the service of dedication.

How then did the sermon become famous among men all over the world if only a handful of Jewish men heard it? Therein lies a true story of brotherhood.

A group of Protestant chaplains who felt that the cancelling of Chaplain Gittelsohn's sermon was unfair secretly got a copy of the address. They had it mimeographed by the thousands and handed it out all over the island. The very act which originally suppressed the sermon was responsible for spreading it far and wide.

Copies of the sermon reached the shores of America where it was read widely. This distribution was a true act of kindness and compassion, one chaplain for another. Some of the Christian chaplains felt that Chaplain Gittelsohn's sermon was so moving that they wanted everyone to read it, even if they could not hear it. This sermon became one of the most famous documents to come out of the War.

As a matter of fact, when Rabbi Gittelsohn delivered the sermon before the Jewish men, those Protestant chaplains were also present. They refused to attend their own denominational service because they insisted on listening to their colleague, the Jewish chaplain.

Just when Rabbi Gittelsohn thought he might lose his faith in brotherhood, he realized that for every man whose heart is poisoned with prejudice and hatred, there are many more who are filled with love of all men, and respect and understanding for men of all faiths.

The Chaplain at Pearl Harbor

ONE BUSY DAY IN THE LIFE OF
RABBI HARRY R. RICHMOND

The time: Sunday morning, December 7, 1943.

The place: Pearl Harbor.

In a sudden, unexpected, sneak attack, the pride of America's Navy went up in blinding smoke. The Japanese had bombed Pearl Harbor.

Death was everywhere. Consuming flames ate up men and ships. Thunderous convulsions shook the entire island, while the world stood up in shocked horror.

Those who survived that day have an indelible impression on their memory of their every movement, every activity, every word spoken. One of those who set his mind's record on paper for following generations is Chaplain Harry R. Richmond, who was stationed there on the day of infamy.

Rabbi Richmond's record of activities on that day is one of acts of mercy, compassion and tender shepherding of his flock. From early morning when the boom first dropped on a quiet serene island, to the dark hours of the night when world history had been irreversibly altered, his hours were filled with serving his men, his country, his God.

Rushing immediately to the hospital at Schofield Barracks, he began to witness the bloody carnage wreaked by the Japanese invaders. To the wounded lying in their beds, he ministered in many ways. Some he handed a cold glass of water to slake their thirst. To others, he expressed a word of hope and encouragement. The American flag was still waving high, he said. The American forces would meet the challenge with compound interest. To ears that could still hear, the chaplain brought some measure of comfort and consolation.

The next task was to bury the dead. First the living, then those who didn't make it. It was a sad mission for Rabbi Richmond. Only a day before these men were walking, singing, dancing, loving. Now, in masses, they went down together to meet their Maker. At the funeral service, none of their relatives or friends were present. The individual man was lost in this mass of horror.

Rows of coffins stretched as far as the eye could see. An American flag draped the mounds of newly dug earth. Rabbi, priest and minister together uttered words of praise for America's first sacrifice on the altar of peace. Prayers were expressed that these valiant and courageous men shall not have died in vain.

Another chore that the chaplain fulfilled, this time with greater pleasure, was helping to inform the folks back home of the good news of those who lived. The wounded and sick asked him to cable their families and tell them they are alive and on the road to recovery.

One seriously wounded patient had heard that his young brother, a flyer in nearby Honolulu, had been killed in action.

He did not know if the rumor were true or not. How could he break the tragic news to his aged mother? Chaplain Richmond kindly consented to investigate the matter, and luckily came up with the good news that the brother was indeed alive, and worried about his older brother at Schofield. The wounded man suddenly came alive and was well on the road to recovery.

Chaplain Richmond was not always able to bring happy news to the wounded soldiers who yearned for more knowledge about their kith and kin. One badly wounded man, who could hardly speak above a whisper, could not rest until a call was put through to a young lady friend who would be anxious to visit and know he was still alive. The call was made, and the woman promised to visit. When it was clear that she was not coming, the chaplain was able to find out that the woman's heart had since been promised to another.

Another important task which fell upon the shoulders of the chaplain was helping families who had been split up in the tumult of the war sirens and scurrying for shelter. Scores of wives and children were hurried off away from danger into safety areas, while husbands and fathers ran to man battle stations. In the safety zones there was a scarcity of light, food, and water, telephones, and other essentials.

Who would tell the men of the whereabouts and safety of their wives and children? Who could inform the families of the fate of their fighting men? This job fell to the lot of the chaplain. He acted as a connecting link between the men in the field and the wives and children whisked off to safety.

In days that followed, there was a flood of cables, air mail special delivery letters and other urgent messages inquiring about the welfare of sons, brothers and husbands. Each inquiry was investigated and answered by return mail. The folks at home could rest a bit more easily knowing that the chaplain would provide the sorely sought for information.

One mother refused to believe that her son was still alive, despite reports that his wounds were not fatal. She had not heard from him and concluded that he must have died of his wounds. The woman wrote the chaplain to get information regarding the burial. It took a trans-Pacific telephone call to set the mother's mind at ease. Only the weakened voice of her living son could reassure her.

Then, of course, there were the men to be served. Those fighting in the field were visited frequently. Through the good offices of the American Red Cross, the chaplains had acquired small gifts to distribute. This was always a welcome relief from the tension of battle. A contact with home. A bit of small pleasure to break up the monotony and seriousness of warfare.

The chaplains also gave out books and pamphlets and other literature. There was a book for every taste, a magazine for every occasion. These welcome gifts lightened the heavy hearts of men whose minds were filled with death and sorrow.

Wherever it was, and whomever he served, Chaplain Richmond was a welcome person on that day of terror and destruction. His presence always meant to the soldier that despite the evil that suddenly burst out upon the world, there was always hope that tomorrow would bring a better day.

A Chaplain Heals a Broken Soul

THE STORY OF THE MILITARY RABBIS AND
THE DP'S

At 2 o'clock one foggy July morning in 1959, an airplane rolled onto the runway of Lydda Airport, near Tel Aviv, Israel. Rabbi Ernest Lorge stepped off.

At that early hour hardly a soul was awake in all of Israel. The plane had been delayed in New York for mechanical reasons and did not arrive at 9 o'clock in the evening as scheduled. Where would the rabbi go? How could he find a taxi amidst the dark and fog? Where could he find a hotel at this late hour?

While trying to figure out what to do, Rabbi Lorge noticed a woman walking towards him from the waiting room.

"Chaplain, how are you?"

The rabbi could not believe his eyes.

"Yes, Chaplain, it is me alright. I have been sitting in the waiting room for hours. I thought perhaps the flight was cancelled. When I found out that you were coming to Israel, I got the flight number and decided to welcome you."

"Miriam," said the chaplain, "I felt so lost and helpless here in the middle of the night, without friend or advisor, in a foreign country. You really saved my life."

"Not really," answered Miriam Cohen, now an Israeli resident. "Not half as much as you saved mine fifteen years ago."

Miriam was only repaying in a small way the great life-saving act performed by Chaplain Lorge, and a host of other military rabbis, for the people who survived Hitler's mass destruction of European Jewry.

The story begins on April 25, 1945, at 4:40 p.m., fourteen years before the meeting of Rabbi Lorge and Miriam Cohen in Israel. At that time there was no Israel. In fact, there was no home for the thousands of Jews who miraculously escaped the gas chambers and ovens where Hitler and his helpers of Nazi Germany destroyed six million Jews.

When the Allied Forces entered victorious into the lands of former Jewish habitation in Europe, they found many of these Jews on the verge of death. They were emaciated, their limbs were like toothpicks, wearing the striped garments of a prisoner, packed together like cattle in Hitler's concentration camps.

Since Hitler had seized all of their homes and possessions, they had nowhere to go. For most of them, there were only one or two surviving relatives. Most of them had lost their parents, their brothers and sisters, and even their children in the attempted genocide by the Nazi madmen. Thus, they were known as Displaced Persons, or D.P.'s, for short.

The invading armies of the Allies did not know exactly how to help these pathetic D.P.'s. It was the most natural thing, they thought, to turn over the job of rehabilitating them to the Jewish chaplains.

On that April afternoon in 1945, Chaplain Lorge received a request from the Army to interview four Jewish refugee girls from a nearby concentration camp.

As he sat and spoke to the girls, he noticed that only three of them spoke to him. The fourth, Miriam Cohen, remained silent. Later, one of the other three explained to him why Miriam refused to speak.

"She has been in a state of shock," one of the girls explained, "since this morning when she found out that her husband was shot by the Nazis just a few hours before the American Army arrived to free the Jews."

Chaplain Lorge took Miriam aside and spoke to her for over an hour, trying to give her hope and courage. Finally, she uttered a few words.

"Thank you, Chaplain. I am grateful to you for taking so much time to speak to me. I have suffered so much during these brutal years; it is hard to believe that anyone really cares anymore. You have given me new hope."

It did not take long for Miriam to return to a healthier frame of mind. With the help of Chaplain Lorge, she was able to regain her confidence and faith in the world and in God as she watched him and others like him devoting themselves unselfishly to helping the D.P.'s.

"I would like to help you in this work, Chaplain," she told the rabbi. "There must be many like me who need not only the spiritual guidance, but other help. I can give that other help."

"I think that there is much to be done, Miriam, and you certainly can be of great service. I will inquire of the military authorities and see if we can receive permission for you to travel with me to other concentration camps and salvage the wrecked lives of our fellow Jews."

It did not take long for Chaplain Lorge to receive this permission. Miriam began to help the chaplain organize food tranports to the D.P. camps and to provide new clothing for them so that they could rid themselves of the hateful prison uniforms forced upon them by the Nazis. She then began to set up schools for their children. In sum, she helped restore their sense of self-respect and well-being.

Many of the people wanted to send letters to their families in other parts of Europe to determine how many of them were still alive. The only mail delivery in existence at the very end of the war was the military mail system. Through the help of the chaplains, Miriam arranged to have the mail of the D.P.'s sent through the military mail system. In this way, they could also write to their families in America and Palestine. This was a great boost to their morale.

After more than a year of working with the D.P.'s, Miriam was informed that her aunt in Belgium wanted Miriam to live with her. Chaplain Lorge arranged transportation for her. Then he wished her a sad farewell.

"Together we have accomplished a great deal, Miriam. We have literally saved the lives of thousands of refugees by giving them food, clothing, and most important of all, renewed hope and confidence to go on living."

"It was not very much, really," answered Miriam. "If you, the military rabbis of the American Army, can do so much for us D.P.'s, we certainly must help ourselves in whatever way we can. Goodbye, Rabbi, and thank you and all of your colleagues. Someday I will have the chance to do something for you. Mark my words."

Rabbi Lorge remembered this promise as he stepped into the automobile of Miriam Cohen Strauss, now married again, and living as a happy citizen of the State of Israel.

"Now you are the Displaced Person, Chaplain, and I am the native. I am here to help you find your way in my country. It took me fourteen years, but I fulfilled my word."

General Eisenhower Saves the Jews

THE STORY OF THE JEWISH CHAPLAIN WHO SERVED UNDER "IKE"

By July, 1945, Chaplain Judah Nadich had been overseas for three years. He had served during that time all over Europe, including Ireland, England, France and elsewhere. The time was coming close when he would soon be discharged and could return to the quiet warmth of his home in Baltimore.

Certain events occurred during that month which would make those last few months of the chaplain's career the most significant of his entire tour of duty. He did not realize at that time that within a few weeks he would suddenly become the most important Jewish Chaplain in the American Armed Forces.

The story begins when President Harry S. Truman sent a

special representative to Europe to investigate rumors that Jews liberated from concentration camps were not receiving proper treatment. The representative was Earl G. Harrison, Dean of the University of Pennsylvania Law School in Philadelphia.

After Dean Harrison's tour of the Displaced Persons camps in several European countries, he notified the War Department in Washington that many people were being badly treated. Some Jews were under guard in the D.P. camps just as they had been before being liberated by the U.S. Army. Also, according to Dean Harrison's report, there was no adequate housing, food or medical care.

When word of the report began to spread through the United States, Jewish leaders became inflamed with anger. Immediately, several leading rabbis sent cables to the Commander of American Forces in Germany, General Dwight D. Eisenhower, to have him correct the situation. They suggested that he appoint a Jewish advisor to supervise the rehabilitation of the Jews who survived Hitler's mass extermination program.

On August 10, 1945, Chaplain Judah Nadich received a telephone call from General Eisenhower.

"Major Nadich," said the general, "I want you to drop everything and come to my headquarters in Frankfurt. I have an important mission for you to accomplish."

"Yes, sir," answered the rabbi. "I'll report immediately."

Within a few days, Chaplain Nadich reported to "Ike." The General told the rabbi that he wanted him to become his personal advisor for Jewish Affairs.

"Chaplain," said the general, "as you well know six million of your people were killed by the Nazis. When we conquered the Germans, we were able to let thousands of people return to their homelands. We are also trying to move the Jews as quickly as possible from the concentration camps into more comfortable accommodations. To do this, we need an outstanding Jewish leader to supervise this project. You must be that man!"

"I shall be honored to assume this position, General." said Rabbi Nadich. "How shall I start?"

"The first thing to do is requisition German houses and hotels into which we shall begin moving the Jews. We have to feed, clothe, and in every way possible help care for these unfortunate people. We have to help the victims of Nazi Germany feel that they are now beginning to rebuild their lives, regain their dignity and self-respect, and restore their health and security."

Together, General Eisenhower and Rabbi Nadich worked on the problem of relocating the D.P.'s and making them feel once again like human beings.

Only a few weeks after Chaplain Nadich assumed his new position as Eisenhower's advisor for Jewish Affairs, the report made by Dean Harrison prior to the appointment of Rabbi Nadich reached the desk of President Truman. He was shocked at the low living conditions of the D.P.'s. Although much of the situation had already been improved before the report reached the President, he was infuriated by what he read and sent General Eisenhower a very strongly-worded letter:

THE WHITE HOUSE
Washington, D. C.

31 August 1945

My dear General Eisenhower:

I have received the report of Dean Harrison. It seems that official government policies are not being carried out in the field.

For example, military officers have been authorized to requisition housing for the displaced persons. Yet, from this report this has not been done yet. Many of the camps are over-crowded and heavily guarded.

I know that you will agree with me that we have a

particular responsibility toward these victims of persecution and tyranny. We must make clear to the German people that we thoroughly abhor the Nazi policies of hatred and persecution. We have no better opportunity to demonstrate this than by the manner in which we treat the survivors remaining in Germany.

I hope you will report to me as soon as possible the steps taken to clean up the conditions mentioned in the report.

I am communicating directly with the British Government to have the doors of Palestine opened to such of these displaced persons as wish to go there.

Very sincerely yours,
HARRY S. TRUMAN

When this letter reached General Eisenhower, he asked Chaplain Nadich if any of these poor living conditions were still in existence and where.

"I am sorry to report, General," said Chaplain Nadich, "that in the Third Army there seems to be little respect for the position of the D.P."

Angrily, the general picked up the telephone. "Get me General Patton immediately," he told his secretary.

"Hello, George," he said a few seconds later. "What is this nonsense about your keeping the Jews under guard, and letting the Germans walk the streets free? Who was our enemy in this war any way? The Jews were the victims, not the conquered enemy."

"What do I care?" said General Patton.

"You had better care," said General Eisenhower, "because I'm telling you to care. Remove these restrictions immediately, and report back to me when it has been accomplished."

"Yes, sir," said Patton and he replaced the phone.

Rabbi Nadich continued to work for General Eisenhower until December of 1945. At that time, a new advisor arrived to take his place, a civilian—Judge Simon Rifkind of New York. After almost four years in the military, Rabbi Nadich could finally return home and see his family.

But he was not to stay long. Some important Jewish leaders convinced him that he was in a unique position to make another great contribution to the Jewish people.

"We want you, Rabbi Nadich," said Rabbi Stephen Wise, an outstanding Jewish spiritual leader in America, "to go on a speaking tour of the United States and overseas, and tell the world what you saw in Europe. Tell them how our brethren who escaped the gas chambers are now in Europe waiting to be helped, to be transported to Palestine, to be fed, clothed and housed. The work will take years to complete. It needs huge sums of money, and the people you tell your story to will have to provide these funds."

Chaplain Nadich toured the world during the entire year of 1946, telling Jews everywhere what he had seen. The people he spoke to contributed over twenty million dollars to aid the survivors of the Nazi massacre. This was one more instance of the ancient custom of Jews to help their brethren in need when a crisis arose.

Chaplain Judah Nadich and General Dwight David Eisenhower, later to become President of the United States, together saved the lives of thousands of Jews. Their story should never be forgotten.

"There, But for the Grace of God..."

A REFUGEE CHAPLAIN RETURNS TO HIS WAR-TORN BIRTHPLACE

"Goodbye, Amy. Take care of the children. I will miss you, you know that. It's something I must do. I've never felt so strongly about anything in my life."

"I know, George. I understand perfectly. I am very proud of you, and happy. We will miss you, and look forward eagerly for your return. Write often."

Chaplain Vida boarded the ship and sailed for Europe. The year was 1945. As he sailed slowly across the Atlantic, his mind was filled with memories.

George Vida was born in Hungary, and studied in Germany. He received his doctorate at the University of Breslau,

45

and was ordained as a rabbi at the Jewish Theological Seminary in Breslau in 1931. He then served a congregation in Czechoslovakia for eight years.

By 1939, things were very dangerous for Jews in Europe. In April of that year, the rabbi and his wife and their infant son fled from the country, leaving a large family of parents, brothers and sisters in Europe. They would never see most of them again. They came to America, on a boat very much like the one on which Rabbi Vida was now a passenger.

"I was saved for a purpose," he thought to himself as his ship sailed for Europe. "The war is now at a close, and there are a half million Jewish Displaced Persons in Europe. I was almost one of them. I must do all in my power to help those who did not die."

Rabbi Vida had lost his father and sister during the war. Both were murdered by the Nazis in Auschwitz gas chambers. He said to himself often, as he read reports of horrors committed by the Nazis, "There, but for the grace of God go I."

In 1943, Rabbi Vida volunteered to become a chaplain in the U.S. Army. Shortly before that he had become an American citizen. Now he was being assigned to serve in Europe. In addition to serving American Jewish soldiers in Europe, he would be able to help the D.P.'s. He did not dare hope to find any of his family alive.

After serving a few months in Europe, he took leave to look up his home town near Budapest. Upon arrival, he went to the offices of the American Joint Distribution Committee, an organization devoted to relief work for refugees. They showed him long lists of names of people whom they knew had survived the mass slaughter of Jews by Hitler.

"These are all people who served in Hitler's Slave Labor Battalions," said the social worker. "That is how they were able to stay alive. They worked to stay alive—like slaves."

Rabbi Vida began to run through the lists, name after name. It was a burdensome task. But just the thought of finding someone alive prodded him to continue, hour after hour. Finally, at the point of exhaustion, he jumped from his chair.

"Andor," he shouted. "Kalmar Andor. My cousin Bandi. We called him Bandi," he explained to the man behind the desk. "We are the same age, and we grew up together in Hungary. Bandi is still alive."

Excitedly, he got into his jeep and travelled to his small home town, driving directly to the old house where his cousin had been born and raised. Bandi, of course was thrilled to see his cousin, and in the uniform of the United States Army.

After a long conversation, the rabbi's cousin casually asked him a question.

"Did you see your brother yet?"

"Brother? Who? Which one? Where?" He could hardly believe his ears.

"Your brother, Imre. He lives in Csongrad, working in the City Hall."

Rabbi Vida drove to Csongrad, and went directly to the City Hall. Not wanting to frighten his brother, he sent a messenger inside with a note—"Your brother is outside, waiting to see you."

The two brothers fell upon each other in flowing tears. A reunion after six years of not being able to send a word to one another. Imre was still as tall as ever, six feet, but thin and pale. His wife and four-year-old son were put to death by the Nazis. His clothing and furniture had been stolen by neighbors while he withered away in the concentration camp. Now he was a shattered man, never again to be whole. He could not bring himself to leave his birthplace, despite all of the tragedy. He could not face the outside world.

Chaplain Vida left Csongrad depressed, yet determined more than ever to give his all in order to help the Displaced Persons, Hitler's victims.

When he came back to his home post, Frankfurt, Germany, he continued to work from dawn to late at night, trying in every way to provide for the needs of the D.P.'s. He was able to get them extra supplies of food by getting special permission to bring the left over food from the Army mess halls to the Jewish community house where many D.P.'s were now living.

One evening, he sent his assistant with the pick-up truck to the mess hall to get the left over food. A short while later, he returned empty-handed.

"They won't give us any more food," said his assistant. "The mess sergeant said that he 'ain't gonna give the Jews any more food.' "

Chaplain Vida drove to the mess hall himself and pleaded with the sergeant. He could not budge him. Finally, he said, "Sergeant, you'll have to come with me. *You* tell those people there won't be any food for them anymore. I can't."

When they arrived at the Jewish community house, the chaplain arose and introduced the sergeant. "Here is the man who helped you to get this food. He has something to tell you."

The sergeant took a good look at the people, and with tears in his eyes, told them, "Don't go away. I'll be back in five minutes with plenty of food for everybody."

In early 1946, Chaplain Vida received a letter from U.S. Army headquarters in Europe. "You are surplus to the needs of the European Theatre and alerted for shipment to the Zone of Interior and subsequent separation from the service."

He had worked hard and done a good job. Now a younger chaplain would replace him. He had served his people and fulfilled his promise to himself. In a short period of time, he had relived the horrors of his youth, and helped see that the suffering of others was lessened.

The memory of his year in Europe, as an American Army officer, would remain with him for the rest of his life.

Rabbi to the Rescue

HOW A JEWISH CHAPLAIN HELPED REFUGEES ESCAPE TO PALESTINE

At the end of the Second World War, thousands of Jewish survivors of Hitler's program of mass murder were left homeless.

Many countries were asked to accept them, but almost none would. The D.P.'s longed to go to Palestine, where they could feel at home at long last. But, at that time, Palestine was under British rule, and the British issued very few entrance visas each year. Some way had to be found to get these D.P.'s into Palestine.

A member of the Jewish community of Palestine had made his way to France and presented a plan to Chaplain Abraham Haselkorn, the American Jewish chaplain serving in Paris. Because the plan was illegal, the meeting between the two men was held in secret.

"There is only one way to get these Jews out of Europe," said the Palestinian Jew. "A very tiny number of Jews is being permitted, with the consent of the British, to go on an American ship to the Holy Land. Once they are on the ship, they are safe. As a Jewish chaplain you will be permitted to go on the ship and say goodbye to the people leaving for Palestine. No one will question you and no one will search you."

"So far so good," answered the chaplain. "What do I do next?"

"Once these people are on board ship, they will not need their exit visas any more. You must take them from them, and bring them back to Paris, where we will distribute them to others. This way, twice as many people can leave France as was originally permitted."

"But this is illegal," answered the chaplain. "How can I as a rabbi permit such a violation of the law?"

"My dear Chaplain," answered the Palestinian, "millions of our brethren have been slain. Thousands more will die if we do not help them find food, clothing, and shelter. No country in the world wants to take them. The only place they will be accepted is in Palestine. As a rabbi, how can you *not* help us in this plan?"

"Well, perhaps you are right," conceded the chaplain. "But let us suppose this plan works and we get them out of France. How can they get into Palestine with the British ships blockading the whole coast?"

"That is the next step, Rabbi. Here too you can be of tremendous help to us."

The chaplain swallowed with difficulty as he awaited explanation of the next step in the illegal plan in which he was to participate. He knew that his help would mean the saving of many human lives, yet he was somewhat uneasy about doing it as an officer in the U.S. Army.

"Go ahead," he said. "Finish telling me what your plan is. It looks as though you've got me persuaded. I'm sticking my neck in a noose, but it will be worth it if we can save Jewish lives."

"O.K.," continued the Palestinian. "Now listen carefully." He glanced out the window to see if anyone was in hearing distance of the house. "There is an underground army in Palestine known as the *Hagana,* the Palestine Defense Underground Army. The Hagna has devised plans to divert the attention of the British ships along the Mediterranean so that illegal transport ships can come near the coast. Then, with rowboats we bring them ashore in the middle of the night, and sneak them off to shelter homes. Things are in such confusion there, that once they are settled no one will know how they arrived or when."

"This sounds like an ingenious plan," responded the rabbi. "But where do I fit in?"

"Your job," said the Palestinian in a whisper, "is to notify the Hagana's headquarters in Tel Aviv when a ship is coming in. Then they can put their plan into action to help the refugees come ashore without being caught by the British."

"How do I do that?" asked the chaplain.

"It's very simple. With the miiltary wire in your office, you must contact our illegal radio station at Toulon, France. From there, the Hagana contact will radio the message in Hebrew to Tel Aviv. Whenever our Paris headquarters has some vital information about a ship on its way to Palestine, we will notify you by sending a messenger to your office. Then you can notify the Toulon radio station in Hebrew. That way no one will understand you."

"I see," said the chaplain. "I'll try it and see how long it will work."

The underground system worked for several weeks. The exit visas were transferred to different groups, and it was arranged for many Jews to leave France and other European countries for Palestine. The Hagana in Tel Aviv was notified, and they helped many to arrive safely.

One night, Chaplain Haselkorn received a message that

was to be relayed to Toulon through the military wire. He sat down to transmit the message, but the transmitter did not work. After examination, it was seen that an essential part of the radio was burned out. It would have to be replaced very quickly because a ship was approaching Palestine. The lives of hundreds of D.P.'s were at stake. If they were caught, the British might blow them right out of the sea. What a terrible fate that would be after escaping the horrors of Nazi terror!

Luckily, a member of Chaplain Haselkorn's congregation, an Army corporal, saved the situation. He was on duty at a medical station that night and had heard about the chaplain's problem. A man came in for medical attention.

"Help me, I'm bleeding," cried the man, a captain in the Signal Corps.

"How did you get so bruised?" asked the corporal.

"You must not tell or I'll be court-martialed." said the captain. "I was in a fight with one of my men."

"You need a shot of penicillin," the corporal told him, "or infection will set in these wounds and you will be deathly ill. I can give out penicillin only if I write it on my reports, and then you will be found out."

"Please help me," said the captain.

Then the corporal noticed that the captain was in the Signal Corps. "I'll make a deal with you, Captain. You get me a certain radio part without letting anyone know about it, and I'll give you this shot of penicillin."

"Well, O.K.," said the captain. "I have no choice."

Later that evening the captain managed to secure the necessary part and secretly slipped it to the corporal. The corporal brought it in the middle of the night to the rabbi, and he installed it in the transmitter.

"What a miracle!" said the rabbi. "You really saved the day!"

The chaplain immediately sat down at the transmitter and

sent the necessary message to Toulon. From Toulon, the secret Hagana agent relayed it to Tel Aviv.

A few weeks later a message came over the wire that the ship of Jewish refugees had arrived safely in Palestine. It was a close call, but worth the effort. Chaplain Haselkorn thanked his lucky stars, and continued to work with his repaired radio transmitter, helping to save the lives and destinies of hundreds of people.

A Chaplain Helps a Chaplain

THE COMMITTEE OF RABBIS FORMED TO HELP OTHER RABBIS

Private Howard Bernards was stationed at Fort Gordon, Georgia early during the Second World War. He was engaged to be married, and the wedding was scheduled for June 3, 1943, only two weeks away.

Howard was hoping to get a three-day leave beginning June 2nd and, after his wedding, to return to the Fort for shipment overseas. One week before the wedding, Howard was called into the orderly room and told that his orders had come a little bit earlier than expected. He would have to ship out on the second of June.

This was a crushing disappointment. He tried in vain to postpone his orders just long enough to stop at home, get married, and then leave. But because of the war, emergency conditions prevailed, and this was impossible. He had to report immediately to the Navy embarkation port in Brooklyn that same day and await shipment.

His fiancée was in California and was not due to arrive for the wedding until the morning of the marriage ceremony. She couldn't possibly make it before he left. Private Bernards turned to his chaplain for help.

"Do you think, Rabbi," said the heavy-hearted soldier, "that we could arrange a wedding over the telephone? This certainly would help matters for my fiancée and myself."

"I'm sorry," said the chaplain. "Jewish law is very specific about this. You must be present with your bride in the sight of two valid witnesses to be married in the Jewish religion."

"Oh, Chaplain, what should I do?" sighed the soldier.

"Let's see," thought the rabbi. "Maybe there is something we can do after all. It's a long shot, but worth looking into. I know that in wartime conditions certain Jewish laws are suspended temporarily. Perhaps we can be given special permission."

"Who can grant this, Rabbi?"

"There is an organization in New York, which I'm sure you've heard about. It's called the National Jewish Welfare Board."

"Sure, Rabbi. They're the ones who gave out the mezuzah I'm wearing around my neck, and gave us the matzos for our Passover Seder last April. Who hasn't heard of the JWB?"

"Well, Howard, the JWB has a special group that helps chaplains in their chapel program. It is known as the Commission on Jewish Chaplaincy. I'll call the director and see what he says."

The chaplain contacted the director of the Commission on Jewish Chaplaincy and explained the problem. The director said that he was very doubtful that it could be approved, but he did not want to accept responsibility for the final decision on his own.

"You know, Chaplain," said the director, "we have been

receiving many questions of Jewish law recently. Now with so many Jewish men fighting in the war, and so many Jewish chaplains serving—about three hundred now—special war conditions require emergency measures for applying Jewish law. We'll have to set up a special committee to handle these questions."

A special law committee was organized under the leadership of the director of the Commission. Three prominent rabbinical scholars were chosen, one from each branch of Jewish life: Orthodox, Conservative and Reform.

At first, many thought it would not work because each of the three men had differing viewpoints on Jewish law—the Orthodox was very strict, the Conservative less so, and the Reform the most liberal.

The committee did function, and very successfully. Even though the three rabbis would not agree under ordinary circumstances, in the emergency wartime situation they each compromised a little so that unanimous decisions could be reached.

Getting back to Private Bernards, late that same evening the committee met for the first time. They examined the question, and agreed that even though these were emergency conditions, this concession could not be made. It would be better for the soldier to wait and have a proper wedding.

Soon the committee was faced with many other problems.

"Suppose," asked the military rabbi assigned to Japan, "a soldier leaves the U.S. on a Thursday morning and arrives twenty-four hours later in Japan. By his calendar, it would then be Friday morning. But since he had crossed the International Date Line, when he arrives, it is now in the midst of the Sabbath day. Is this soldier to observe the Sabbath as it was for him in New York or in accordance with the local date for the Sabbath?"

The committee of rabbis of the JWB worked on this question very diligently. They studied all of the Jewish law codes very carefully. After a thorough search, they concluded that the question had never really been answered by past rabbis. Thus, they advised, since the International Date Line is accepted by everyone today, it is best to go along with the prevailing custom. A soldier will, therefore, be correct if he observes the Sabbath of the calendar according to local reckoning in Japan.

Another question brought to the attention of the JWB concerned soldiers in areas of the Arctic zones—Iceland, for example.

A Jewish chaplain in Iceland was puzzled about when to begin his Friday evening services because he could not determine when the Sabbath began. Certainly this seems to be simple enough. It is very clearly written in Jewish law that the Sabbath begins when the sun goes down. But in Iceland, it often happens that the sun never goes down! It could be daytime for a month or two, or even six. "Does this mean," asked the rabbi, "that we are not to observe the Sabbath for this whole period of several months?"

The committee solved this question by referring the rabbi to a question similar to that one mentioned in the Talmud, the collection of Jewish writings from the first centuries of the Common Era.

The Talmud relates the story of a man travelling in the desert who lost count of the days. He did not know when the Sabbath was due to fall. Hence, he could not observe it on the right day, except by an excellent guess.

The suggestion given for this man in the Talmud was as follows: He should begin counting days immediately, and observe every seventh day as the Sabbath, whether it actually is or not.

The committee explained that while this situation does not exactly parallel the present problem, it does give much guidance. From the Talmud's answer, they understood that in a case in which one is not sure about the time of the Sabbath's arrival, he can choose a certain fixed time and observe that as the Sabbath even though he is not fully sure it is the Sabbath.

Thus, the committee answered the chaplain by advising him to select the hours of the Sabbath as it is observed in New York, even though it does not get dark. In this way, he will have a fixed basis, his own watch, to know when to begin and end the Sabbath, even though he is not using the traditional method of judging from the setting of the sun.

These, and many other answers like them, helped the military rabbi to observe faithfully the dictates of the Jewish religion in the midst of war's perils and strains.

The Flying American Rabbi

THE STORY OF FLIGHT PILOT SHMUEL BARAV
(Alias Rabbi Samuel Burstein)

In one of the camps for Displaced Persons in Europe, a tall, thin man sat in the corner of a room with a blanket protecting him from the cold. It was October, 1948.

At the other side of the room was another D.P. who could not take his eyes off the man in the corner, known as David Szupack.

"Mr. Szupack," he said, "you look terribly familiar. Where have I seen you before? Perhaps you lived near me in Berlin before the war?"

"No, I doubt it," said Mr. Szupack. "I have never lived in Berlin. You must be mistaking me for someone else."

"No, I am not," said the man. "I know you from somewhere, and it seems to me that I have seen you very very recently."

An American Army official was standing at the door, listening to the conversation. Then he stepped outside. When Mr. Szupack saw him leave, a broad smile began to cover his face. He took off his hat, and removed the blanket from around his chin. "Now do you recognize me?" he asked the other D.P.

"Chaplain Burstein! What are you doing in torn clothing in a D.P. camp?"

"Sh! Not so loud," said Mr. Szupack, alias Rabbi Samuel Burstein.

"Why, just two weeks ago you were our supervisory chaplain, and now this. Please explain it to me!" said the D.P. in complete shock and surprise.

By this time, all of the other D.P.'s in the camp had gathered around to listen to the story.

"You see," began the rabbi, "the job of the so-called 'D.P. Chaplain' serving with the Army in Europe to help displaced Jews is now being taken over by civilian organizations. So just a few weeks ago I resigned my commission in the U.S. Army, since I felt that I was not needed anymore."

"Fine," interrupted one of the listeners. "But why didn't you go back to America to your synagogue in Lincoln, Nebraska?"

"It is very simple," replied the chaplain. "You know that only a few months ago, last May in fact, the State of Israel was proclaimed by David Ben Gurion in Tel Aviv. After two thousand years of oppression and persecution, our people finally has its own free, sovereign and independent nation. I want to be a part of this great venture."

Another D.P. spoke up. "But I heard that the Arabs are attacking from all sides, seven Arab nations at once. What can a rabbi do at such a time? Who has time for services?"

"There is much that a rabbi can do in such a perilous time," answered Chaplain Burstein. "But it is not as a rabbi that I want to serve in Israel. You see, while I was a rabbi in Nebraska I learned how to fly a plane in my spare time at the Union Air Service. I want to be a pilot in the Israeli Air Force."

When the listeners regained their composure after hearing this amazing tale, they continued to question the former U.S. Army chaplain.

"Why can't you just go to Israel directly? Why the disguise, and why the new name?"

"Because the UN forbids it," answered Chaplain Burstein. "No men of fighting age are permitted entrance into Israel to fly war planes. Rabbi Burstein felt that if he could enter. It is the perfect disguise."

Yes, it was true. A rabbi from Nebraska was going to Israel to fly war planes. Rabbi Burstein felt that if he could not help Israel survive in this great hour of crisis, he was not doing his share for the Jewish people.

When the chaplain arrived in Israel, as Mr. Szupack, he changed his name to Shmuel Barav, using his real Hebrew first name and making his own last name, Burstein, sound authentically Hebrew. Samuel Burstein had now become Shmuel Barav.

After being in Israel only a few days, Rabbi Samuel Burstein, alias David Szupack, alias Shmuel Barav, joined the Israeli Air Force.

While standing in the recruiting line, he happened to chat with the man in front of him to pass the time away.

"Are you an Israeli?" asked the man in front of him.

"No," said Barav. "I am an American. Are you Israeli?"

"Yes, I am," answered the future pilot. "But if you are not, you better not take the oath when you reach the front of the line."

"Why not?" asked pilot Barav in amazement. "If I don't swear allegiance to the State of Israel, I won't be accepted into the Air Force."

"If you do, my good friend, you will lose your citizenship

in the United States. You can fight with our Armed Forces and still maintain your citizenship in America, but you can't take an oath of allegiance to our government. If you do, you will never see the U.S.A. again."

"What shall I do then?" asked Barav.

"There is a special oath you can take. Ask the recruiter about it when you get to the front of the line. He won't ask you about it, but if you make a special request, he will let you take the special oath for foreigners. It will not commit you like the Israeli oath does."

"When Barav reached the front of the line and explained his position to the recruiter, he was able to take the following oath: "I will pledge that I will follow the orders of superior officers, and I will not reveal any military secrets."

"O.K.," said the recruiter. "You are now Flight Officer #115352."

"Thanks to #115351," thought Rabbi Burstein to himself, "I can still maintain my precious right of being an American citizen."

Flight Officer Shmuel Barav became Commanding Officer of the Beer Sheba Air Base, and flew several very successful missions in the Negev Desert. He performed an outstanding service to the Israeli nation and the Jewish people as a whole.

A year and a half after his first flight as an Air Force pilot in July, 1949, he received a radio message from a small military outpost at Sodom. A man had been killed by an Arab bullet, and there was no rabbi to perform the funeral ceremony. Barav quickly got into his plane and flew to Sodom and performed the funeral. He recited the prayers from his little prayerbook, which he had carried with him from the United States, through Germany, and now to the Negev Desert. It served him well.

Thus, Shmuel Barav was the only rabbi in history to fly on his own wings to conduct a funeral.

In January, 1951, after the hostilities had ended, Barav became a teacher in the Air Force Pilots School. He taught mathematics, physics, and aerodynamics. In fact, he even composed Hebrew manuals and courses of study for these courses for future instructors.

One day after class, he met an American tourist named Pearl Shmidman. She was the daughter of an American rabbi from New York. After a period of courtship, the two became engaged. In July, 1951, they returned to the U.S. to get married.

In the U.S. many people asked Rabbi Burstein why he chose to leave the rabbinate for four years and serve as a pilot.

"It helped me to be closer to God," he answered. "Besides, I was able to be of great service to our people in this time of crisis. Now that the war is over, and I have done my share, I can resume my main job in life. After all, it is very difficult to direct an aircraft. But it is infinitely easier than trying to guide opinion and develop character. This is the real challenge of my life, one that I want to return to."

Postscript

Rabbi Burstein (not Barav anymore) is now the Rabbi of Temple Beth Israel, Port Washington, New York.

Bar Mitzvah for 28 Boys at Once

THE STORY OF CHAPLAIN GORRELICK WITH JEWISH ORPHANS IN BELGIUM

For six months after World War II, Chaplain Benjamin H. Gorrelick was stationed in Brussels, Belgium. June, 1945 to January, 1946 were to become the most rewarding six months of his entire life.

Shortly after he arrived in Brussels, Rabbi Gorrelick was taken to the several Jewish orphanages in the city, housing 2,000 boys and girls whose parents had been killed by the Nazis. The youngsters ranged in age from infants to teenagers.

Chaplain Gorrelick would visit the orphanages often, bringing American GIs with him. The GIs were looked upon as saviors for having conquered the enemy, and the children thrilled with excitement every time the chaplain and his soldiers came to visit.

Since the war had just ended, there was not yet any clothing, food or medicine for the people of Belgium. These vital needs of the orphaned children were left unfulfilled.

Chaplain Gorrelick came upon an idea. He wrote to his wife in Albany, New York, where the rabbi's congregation was located, and he asked her to organize a committee to send packages of food, clothing and medicine to Belgium.

Packages began pouring in by the hundreds. In fact, every single week for months over a hundred packages arrived for the chaplain. After a while the Post Office officials began to get suspicious. One day, for example, every single piece of mail that arrived at the Post Office was addressed to the "Jewish Chaplain." Some of the packages were damaged on the way overseas. Beans, peas, flour, pills and crumbs were leaking from the sides.

"I bet this chaplain is running an illegal blackmarket operation," exclaimed one of the postal officials.

The next thing he knew, the chaplain was summoned to report to his Commanding General to explain the mysterious influx of hundreds of packages of food and pills. After a brief explanation, the general understood and sympathized.

"However," said the general, "even though what you are doing is a good thing, it is against the regulations. I am afraid you will have to put a stop to it."

Chaplain Gorrelick left the general's office greatly angered and disappointed. What could he tell the orphaned Jewish children who relied on him for all of the good things they had been receiving for so long?

One of the GIs in his congregation gave the chaplain an excellent idea.

"Why don't you write your wife, Chaplain," said the soldier, "and give her the names and addresses of a group of us soldiers? Then she can mail some of the packages to each of us. She will no longer have to send all of them in your name. In that way it will not look suspicious."

"An excellent idea," responded the rabbi. "That's exactly

what we'll do. Go now and ask for as many names and addresses among the men as you possibly can."

Only a few hours later, the soldier came back with dozens of names of soldiers who would be willing not only to receive the packages for the orphans, but to deliver them personally to the orphanage.

Every time the chaplain drove his military jeep near the orphanage the children would run outside to greet him. "Monsieur Le Chaplain!" they shouted as they saw him in the distance.

On one particular occasion, all of the children ran up to the chaplain's jeep, jumped onto the vehicle, and climbed all over him.

"Chaplain, Chaplain," they screamed. "We want to be Bar Mitzvah. Please let us become Bar Mitzvah."

When the commotion settled down, the chaplain asked the children why all of a sudden they wanted to become Bar Mitzvah.

One of the older boys was the spokesman for the group. "Rabbi, Joseph received a letter from his cousin in America today describing his Bar Mitzvah. We want to have a ceremony like that. Since you are an American rabbi, can you have us Bar Mitzvah in a nice ceremony like Joseph's cousin's?"

The chaplain sat in his jeep and smiled. "Why haven't you older boys been Bar Mitzvah already? A boy should be Bar Mitzvah when he is age thirteen," said the chaplain.

"We wanted to," said the spokesman, "but it was impossible. When we reached the age of thirteen, our country was occupied by the Nazis, and they did not permit any religious services. We had to hide in our houses, because if they found us we would have been killed like our parents. Our mothers and fathers promised us a nice Bar Mitzvah when the war was over, but now they are not here to do it. Will you help us, Chaplain?"

"Of course I will," answered the chaplain. "I think that it

is wonderful that you want to be Bar Mitzvah, and I am sure your parents would be proud of you if they were living today."

And so, Chaplain Gorrelick wrote to his congregation in Albany, and twenty-eight sets of *talit* and *tefillin* were sent, together with a copy of the *Siddur* (the Jewish prayerbook). For several weeks, the rabbi taught the group how to wear the *tallit* and the *tefillin* and how to recite the special *berakhot* (benedictions) that had to be recited over them. Finally, the day of the mass Bar Mitzvah arrived.

Twenty-eight young Jewish boys, ranging from fourteen to seventeen years old, who had been denied the privilege of a Bar Mitzvah at age thirteen, now had the chance to fulfill that wish.

That Bar Mitzvah ceremony was a symbol for the Jews of Belgium that the end had finally come to the horrors of Nazi rule, and that a free and normal life was beginning once again.

Passover in Goebbels' Castle

CHAPLAIN JOSEPH S. SHUBOW CROSSES
GERMANY'S "RED SEA"

In the last months of World War II, Chaplain Joseph S. Shubow, serving in the Ninth United States Army in Germany, was discussing Passover with his men.

"In only a few weeks," he told them, "we shall be celebrating our ancient Festival of Freedom, commemorating the time when Moses and the Israelites went out of Egypt."

"Perhaps," suggested one Jewish soldier, "God will be good to us and bring us to complete victory, as he did with Moses at the Red Sea."

These words were prophetic. The very next day, the Ninth Army, under the leadership of Major General John P. Anderson, began to cross the Rhine River.

"Rabbi," said the general to Chaplain Shubow, "is it not

remarkable that we are crossing the Rhine only a short time before Passover, when you commemorate the crossing of the Red Sea, which took place thousands of years ago?"

"Yes, it is," answered the rabbi. "One of the men in the division I serve remarked only yesterday that perhaps God will redeem us and grant us victory, just as he did to Moses at the Red Sea."

When Rabbi Shubow told his men what General Anderson had said, they laughed. To think that what a Jewish soldier said to his chaplain was the very same thought expressed by a two-star general!

This was the first of two things which made that Passover different from any the Jewish men in the Ninth Army had ever celebrated before.

Rabbi Shubow wanted very much to make this Passover one that his "boys" would never forget. The historic circumstance of being in Germany during the war at Passover season was one that he knew held great possibilities for making the holiday especially meaningful. He felt the deep meaning of the Festival of Freedom very personally. He felt that he was living in an age when a tyrant even more wicked than Pharoah held power over many people. To end the rule of this tyrant, as Pharoah's rule had ended long ago, would be a great triumph.

About a week later, Chaplain Shubow was driving around the vicinity of Muenchen Gladback, trying to find an appropriate place to hold the Passover Seder.

"Is there a large hall in this area," he asked one of the local German residents, "that could be used for a festival dinner for several hundred men?"

"None that I know of," was the answer he received again and again.

Finally, after driving around all day, one kind resident offered good advice to the rabbi.

"Ach ja, es gibt doch Goebbels Schloss in der Nahe." (Oh yes, Goebbels' castle is in the vicinity.)

Goebbels was one of the leaders of Nazi Germany, and was largely responsible for the massacre of countless Jewish people. The thought of holding a Passover Seder in Goebbels' castle gave the rabbi a special delight.

Chaplain Shubow located the castle on his map and drove there immediately. He found a Colonel Barney Oldfield, press officer of the Ninth Army, in charge of the castle.

"I would like to use this castle," said the chaplain, "for our Passover Seder this year. Do you think there will be any objection to that?"

"Would you repeat that, please, Chaplain?"

"We would like to use Goebbels' castle for our Passover Seder. Since it is now in American hands, we don't see why we cannot make use of it for our religious celebration."

"Don't get me wrong, now, Chaplain," replied the colonel, with a look of shock and amazement on his face. "I don't want to stop you in any way. In fact, I think it would be a sensational idea. It just kind of took me by surprise."

"Well, that's easy to understand," retorted Rabbi Shubow. "It isn't every day that a Jewish festival meal is held in the former living quarters of a leading Nazi!"

"You know, Rabbi," said Colonel Oldfield, "I come from Hollywood. In my neck of the woods this kind of story could make a million dollars. If I were a script writer, I would make a movie out of your Passover Seder. I can see it now. Here is how we would advertise it—'Jewish Passover is Celebrated by a Jewish Chaplain and American Jewish Soldiers in Goebbels' Castle.' If I were to write a fictional story about such an event, they would never believe it."

"Well, can we have the castle or not?" asked the rabbi. "I can't wait around all day while you write your Hollywood scripts, you know."

"You sure can have it, with all my blessings. And may the Almighty grant you and your men the happiest Passover of their lives."

"Thank you, Colonel. I'm sure the message of this Passover

will not be lost on anyone. All of us will appreciate it more than we can tell you. For it will demonstrate to us once again that no tyrant can stand in the path of freedom. From Pharaoh to Hitler and Goebbels, history has shown us that wickedness and hatred will never prevail."

Passover was never so sweet as it was for the Jewish men of the Ninth Army in Goebbels' castle, April, 1945.

Six weeks later the Russian army closed in on Berlin, and Goebbels took his own life.

The prophetic words of the young soldier the day before he crossed the Rhine came back to the chaplain and the general. Divine redemption had shown itself once again.

A Chaplain Plays Archeologist

CHAPLAIN HAROLD SAPERSTEIN DISCOVERS SOME ANCIENT JEWISH TREASURES

In the spring of 1945, Chaplain and Mrs. Harold Saperstein left their quarters in the Vosges mountains of France and traveled to Worms, the historic ancient city of Germany.

Chaplain Saperstein had heard about a famous handwritten *machzor* (High Holy Day prayerbook) from the 13th century which was kept in the synagogue at Worms. He wanted to find out if it were still in existence.

It was not hard to find the famous synagogue of Worms. It was an historic shrine. Built in the year 1034, it was used by the famous Rabbi Solomon ben Yitzchak (known as *Rashi* after the initials of his Hebrew name).

Alas, the synagogue was now in ruins. Seven years before, in November 1938, the Germans in one night destroyed 500

72

synagogues in Germany and France, including this one. This happened on the infamous *Krystallnacht*, or Night of Broken Glass, called such because of the smashing destruction committed by the Nazis.

After visiting the destroyed synagogue, Chaplain Saperstein went to the local Museum of Worms and spoke to its curator, Dr. Illert.

"You know, Dr. Illert," said the rabbi, "the synagogue at Worms possessed a great many treasured manuscripts and ritual objects. One of them in particular was extremely valuable. That is a hand-written prayerbook dating back to the 13th century. Would you possibly know if it was destroyed with the synagogue in 1938 during *Krystallnacht?*"

"No, as a matter of fact," replied the curator, "I have it right here in the Municipal Museum."

Chaplain Saperstein could not believe his ears. "How did this happen?" asked the chaplain.

"I had a feeling that something drastic was going to happen to the synagogue that night; so I took the *machzor* and placed it here for safekeeping."

Dr. Illert took the rabbi and his wife, and another chaplain travelling with them, down to the basement of the museum building, where the town archives were kept. He lifted up the two heavy volumes of the *machzor* and handed them to the chaplains.

"Look," said Chaplain Saperstein to his friend, "the writing is still in excellent condition."

"Yes," replied the other chaplain, "the colored illumination is still clear and beautiful. The pages are stained with age."

As the men stared at the old prayerbook, they thought of the many generations of pious Jews who had prayed from that *machzor* on the Holy Days.

The chaplains took the *machzor* and turned it over to the Military Government in Germany. When the war was over, it found its way to the National Library of the Hebrew

University in Jerusalem, where it is still preserved today. Visitors who pass through the library's treasured Manuscript Room can see it on view in a beautiful case.

While talking to Dr. Illert, Chaplain Saperstein discovered some additional information.

"After the synagogue began to burn that night," the curator told the chaplains, "I rushed over there and tried to salvage whatever I could. I managed to save some of the Torah scrolls, even though they were burned badly, and some of the precious ritual items in the synagogue's museum."

"Where are these things now, Dr. Illert?" asked the chaplain.

"At the time, seven years ago, I placed them in large metal boxes, and brought them down to the basement of the museum. Unfortunately, that part of the museum was also destroyed by a bomb. The roof and floor caved in and buried the boxes under tons of debris."

"You know," said Chaplain Saperstein, "it is worth a try to see if we can find these boxes. Can we get a crew of diggers here to start working?"

Dr. Illert was very cooperative in trying to obtain the services of a digging crew. The very next day the men started digging through the ruins to find the precious metal boxes.

The work took several days. Every few hours Chaplain Saperstein would go down to the basement and see how the diggers were progressing.

Finally, on the fourth day of digging, towards evening, one of the shovels hit something with a metallic sound.

As soon as he heard that sound, Chaplain Saperstein grabbed a shovel and jumped into the hole created by the diggers.

"Move aside," he told the men. "I have to finish this myself."

After a few minutes of digging, he uncovered two trunk-like metal containers. He dismissed the workmen, and sat in the hole with the boxes. Opening them, he took out the precious objects one by one, handling them with loving care.

Among them were three Torah scrolls. It was dark, and hence difficult to read. Chaplain Saperstein took out a small flashlight from his pocket and focused it on the Torah scroll.

He tried to read the passage, even amidst great darkness. Finally, after studying it for several minutes, he was able to decipher the writing. The passage was from the book of Deuteronomy:

"When you go forth to battle against your enemies, and see horses and chariots and a people more numerous than you, do not fear them, for the Lord your God is with you."

The Secret Message
about Horseradish

CHAPLAIN MICHAEL D. GELLER AND
OPERATION PASSOVER

It was only seven days till Passover, 1952. Michael D. Geller, the Jewish chaplain at Air Force Headquarters, Texas, was busy preparing for the Seder.

While sitting at his desk that afternoon, Chaplain Geller received an urgent phone call.

"Hello, is this Chaplain Geller?"

"Yes, it is."

"This is the MARS Radio Station on post. There is an emergency high priority message for you from Ramey Air Force Base in Puerto Rico," said the voice on the other end.

"Read it to me quickly," answered the chaplain.

"I am afraid, sir, that I can't make it out. It seems to be in code. It is probably a secret message that is written in code because of its classified nature."

"Well, then, can you spell it out?" asked the chaplain.

"Yes, sir, I can. Here it is: "P" "E" "S" "A" "C" "H" . . . .

Chaplain Geller copied out the message, letter by letter. Finally, he saw what it said:

"PESACH SEDER SUPPLIES—NO CHRAIN-GE-FILTA"

The message was clear. The Jewish chaplain at Ramey Air Force Base, Puerto Rico, was short of supplies for his Passover Seder.

Chaplain Geller dropped everything and summoned his assistant to bring the jeep around to the front of the chapel.

"We're going on an emergency mission," he told the young soldier. "Operation Horseradish."

On the way to Shreveport, Louisiana, the chaplain explained the situation to his assistant.

"The rabbi at the Air Force Base in Puerto Rico probably got a new group of Jewish men all of a sudden, and had no way of receiving his Passover Seder supplies. He must have run short of horseradish (*chrain* in Yiddish), and gefilte fish, two very necessary ingredients for a Passover Seder."

"I see," said the assistant. "And since he is so far away from any large Jewish community, he must order his Pesach supplies weeks or even months in advance."

"Exactly right," answered the chaplain. "Not everyone is as fortunate as we are to have a Jewish delicatessen nearby."

The chaplain and his assistant purchased three one gallon jars of horseradish and a large supply of gefilte fish. They wrapped it all very carefully, and labelled the box "To the Jewish Chaplain, Ramey Air Force Base, Puerto Rico." Then, under that, the chaplain wrote in large red letters: "Religious Articles—Very Holy and Very Important. Handle with Great Care."

The next problem was to get the cartons to Puerto Rico

in time for Passover. With only a week to go, certainly the regular mails could not be used.

Chaplain Geller sat down in his office and picked up the telephone.

"Give me Flight Operations, please. Hello, Flight Operations," he said. "What kind of plane do you have going in the vicinity of Ramey in Puerto Rico?"

"Nothing directly there, sir," was the reply. "But we do have something going to MacDill Air Force Base in Tampa, Florida. Will that help?"

"I'll call you right back," said the chaplain.

"O.K., sir, but the plane leaves in twenty minutes. You'll have to let me know soon."

The chaplain ordered his assistant to put the packages in the jeep and get right over to the plane leaving for Florida.

"Put the packages on that plane within twenty minutes," he told his assistant. "Then just as the plane is ready to take off, call me, and I'll tell you whether to let it go or not."

"Will do, sir," said the assistant, as he ran out the door without even saying goodbye.

Then Chaplain Geller called the Base Chaplain at MacDill in Tampa, Florida.

"Chaplain," he asked, "do you have any flights going to Ramey in Puerto Rico within the next few days?"

"I'm not sure, but I'll find out right away and call you back."

Meanwhile, Rabbi Geller sat at his desk wondering whether his package would make it to the plane in time to reach MacDill.

A few short minutes later, the phone rang. "This must be the chaplain at MacDill," thought Chaplain Geller to himself.

But it wasn't. It was the chaplain's assistant. "The package is on the plane, and they're ready to roll. Should I let it go?"

"Oh, no," answered Chaplain Geller. "I haven't heard from MacDill yet. What's your number? I'll call you there as soon as I hear from Tampa. Meanwhile, see if you can hold the plane."

No sooner had the chaplain replaced the receiver in the cradle when the phone rang again.

"This is the chaplain at MacDill," said the speaker. "We have a plane going to Ramey on Thursday morning. Will that make it in time?"

"Let's see, Passover is on the 18th, that's Friday night. That's perfect. Can you see that a certain package I'll send you gets on the plane?"

"I'll do my best," said the chaplain at MacDill.

Chaplain Geller called his assistant and told him to let the package fly with the plane to Tampa.

About twenty minutes later, the soldier returned and reported to Chaplain Geller: "Mission Accomplished. The chrain and gefilte fish are on their way to MacDill."

Six days later, Friday morning before the Seder, Chaplain Geller received another call from the MARS Radio Station. Another classified message.

"CHRAIN ARRIVED B'SHOLOM. CHAG SAMEACH AND A KOSHER PESACH."

The Chaplain translated it to the MARS Radio Operator: "The horseradish arrived safely. Happy holiday and a Kosher Passover."

The Boy in Bed Sixteen

CHAPLAIN HOWARD D. SINGER IN KOREA

In late December, 1952, Chaplain Howard D. Singer was making his routine rounds at the Air Force Hospital in Seoul, Korea. He expected that it would be a day like any other day. He would offer a word of cheer to one wounded pilot. To another he would distribute a trinket sent from home to keep the airman's mind off his wound.

But this day was to turn out to be one he would remember for a long time.

As he entered the hospital, he stopped in to chat with his friend, Captain Leopold, the Air Force physician.

"I'm happy that you stopped in here today, Chaplain, before going through the wards."

"You know I never go directly into seeing the patients before I speak to you, Bob."

"You know, Rabbi Singer, that I always tell you to go right through and greet the men, and offer them whatever good words you can. But today, I must confess that I have a problem."

"What seems to be different on this occasion, Bob?" queried the chaplain, with a look of surprise on his face.

"I am sure that most of the men will be thrilled to see you, Chaplain, as they always are. But I feel it necessary to warn you about one new patient."

"Which one, Bob, and why?"

"Well, Chaplain, if I were you I would politely skip the man in bed sixteen."

The chaplain's curiosity grew as he listened to the rest of the story.

"That kid is an amputee. He had both arms blown off in combat, and was recently transferred here. He was married a few months before being shipped out. And now this."

"If you say so, Doctor. Sometimes it is just better to leave someone alone if he is not anxious for company."

"I would, Chaplain. He has made it awfully difficult for the nurses. He gets itchy every time someone tries to talk to him or do anything for him. He's one guy I don't think even a chaplain can help right now."

Fully intending to take the advice of Dr. Leopold, Rabbi Singer strolled down the aisle, from bed to bed, saying hello and inquiring into the health and welfare of each wounded serviceman.

When he came closer to bed sixteen he began to walk a bit faster, and cast a glance at bed seventeen, preparing to strike up a conversation with its occupant. But suddenly, he stopped in his tracks. He didn't know what it was, but for some reason, he could not move any further. Reaching bed seventeen, he stepped back a few paces . . . slowly. Then, he turned his head around and looked at the man in number sixteen.

He stood for a moment and stared, embarrassed. Should

he move on, as he promised the captain at the desk, or should he take just a minute and stop at the bed of the amputee?

Noticing that bed fifteen was unoccupied, he walked over and sat down. Looking at the patient in sixteen, he saw a handsome, young fellow, with dark black hair. The boyish-looking airman was sitting up in bed, half propped up, with his blanket tucked in right up to his neck. He was staring straight at the blank wall on the other side of the room.

Chaplain Singer sat there for a moment, reaching for the right thing to say. Somehow, it did not come. A heavy silence lay on the room. The young wounded man did not even turn to say hello, or notice that he had company.

After several minutes of being uncomfortable, the patient turned to the chaplain and looked at his insignia: The tablets of the ten commandments with a Star of David sitting on top.

"You are a chaplain, aren't you, Lieutenant Singer?"

"That's right. The Jewish chaplain," answered the rabbi, groping for something to say.

Without looking at the chaplain directly, he spoke to him. "Do you think it's wrong to hate, Chaplain?"

"I don't think it's a good idea," said Rabbi Singer, "but I can't blame you at the moment. My job is not to tell people how to feel."

"You know, Chaplain, it's not easy to have people clamber all over, not knowing how to treat me. Either they're so cheerful that you might think nothing happened, or they're so full of pity that they make me sick."

The young man then turned directly to the chaplain, "Must it always be like this?"

"No, not necessarily. It really depends on you most."

"What do you mean?"

"Look," said Chaplain Singer. "It all boils down to your attitude. You set the pace. If you give the impression to others and have a look on your face as if you wish you were dead, they will pity you forever. If you try to pass it off too lightly, people will pretend to be cheerful and overly mirthful."

"Well, then, what *am* I supposed to do?"

"Act just how you feel."

"If I do that, it means I must act miserable."

"O.K., then act miserable. It's only natural. You've had a rotten break. Anybody in your position would feel the same. But eventually you've got to start looking at things realistically. Of course, things will never be exactly the same. You've had a very bad injury, which will cause you tremendous difficulties for the rest of your life. But, after a while, things will be better than you can imagine right now."

The boy sat quietly and listened. For a while, there was no answer. Finally, the chaplain broke the second silence.

"Do you want me to go?" asked Rabbi Singer, getting up from bed fifteen.

"No, Not you. I suppose I need someone here after all."

The chaplain sat there for almost an hour, continuing to talk to his newly-acquired friend. When he finally got up to leave, the young man said to him: "I'll be O.K., Chaplain. Don't worry. I'll be O.K. Just make sure to come again. You'll see."

The Mystery of Nagasaki's Vanished Jews

CHAPLAIN TOKAYER TRACES A HIDDEN JEWISH CEMETERY

In the search for an old Jewish cemetery in Nagasaki, Japan, Chaplain Marvin Tokayer searched all over the Far East. He spoke to people in Nagasaki, Kobe, Tokyo, Seoul, and Hong Kong.

Chaplain Tokayer served in the Air Force as a roaming Jewish chaplain, from 1962-1964. Since there were Jews stationed in the Army, Navy, and Air Force, all over Japan, he had to travel from place to place to find them and serve them.

Once during a trip to Kobe, Japan, Chaplain Tokayer met a man named Jacob Gottlieb, born in Russia and now in the import-export business in Kobe.

"You know, Chaplain," said Mr. Gottlieb, "you ought to visit the old cemetery in Nagasaki and see if the Jewish graves are being cared for properly."

"A Jewish cemetery in Nagasaki?" said the startled chaplain. "I didn't know there was one! Who is taking care of it?"

"I don't know," answered Mr. Gottlieb. "After these many years, I don't even know if anyone has so much as stepped inside its gates."

"A Jewish cemetery being so neglected!" said the chaplain, gasping in surprise. "That is against Jewish custom. Graves must be cared for. Jewish law demands respect for the dead. I must find the cemetery and see that it is cared for. I know! . . . I'll ask the Jews of Nagasaki. They'll tell me where it is."

"That would be simple enough," answered the merchant. "The unfortunate thing is that there are no Jews there today. They all left Nagasaki in 1920 for Tokyo and Kobe."

"How long had they been there?" he asked Mr. Gottlieb.

"For about a thousand years," answered the merchant. "Jewish merchants came here from many countries long, long ago, along with their Christian companions."

After speaking to Mr. Gottlieb in Kobe, Chaplain Tokayer was determined to find the Jewish cemetery and see that the graves were cared for properly. He also wanted to shed light on the history of the Jewish community that lived in Nagasaki, about which apparently no one knew anything at all.

"Where do you recommend I start this search?" the chaplain asked Mr. Gottlieb.

"If my memory serves me correctly," said Mr. Gottlieb, "the records of the synagogue of Nagasaki have been sent to Shanghai. Perhaps some clue to the whereabouts of the cemetery can be found in these records."

On his next trip to Shanghai, Chaplain Tokayer looked for the records, but could not find them. The answer would have to be found elsewhere.

On a trip to Korea a short time later, the rabbi met

two Russian-born Jews who engaged him in conversation. They told him about a man in Tokyo who might be able to furnish him with more information.

"You ought to look up Mr. Lurie, a motion picture distributor in Tokyo," they told him.

Thus, it was off to Tokyo for Chaplain Tokayer. He searched out Mr. Lurie and arranged an appointment with him.

"There certainly was a Jewish Community in Nagasaki," said Mr. Lurie. "I myself was born there! My parents had come there earlier from America to find business opportunities."

"Was there a synagogue there and a cemetery?" asked the rabbi eagerly.

"Yes, there was a synagogue and a cemetery," was the answer. "The Jews of Nagasaki were involved in selling supplies to visiting ships. Around forty years ago they all moved to Tokyo and Kobe."

Having gathered all of these pieces of information, Rabbi Tokayer now knew much more about the vanished Jews of Nagasaki than he did before. But he still did not have enough information to find the lost cemetery.

On his next trip to Hong Kong, Chaplain Tokayer met a Dr. Cohen, who had also lived in Nagasaki originally. Now the chaplain felt himself getting closer to his goal.

"I have relatives who were buried in the cemetery at Nagasaki," Dr. Cohen told the chaplain. "I used to visit there often until the A-bomb fell. I felt sure that the synagogue and cemetery were destroyed, and I haven't been there since."

Just when his hopes for finding the cemetery were the highest, Chaplain Tokayer learned that he might never find it. Perhaps Dr. Cohen was right. It may have been totally destroyed by the United States' atomic bombing. In any case, he asked Dr. Cohen for directions to the cemetery, as well as he could remember.

On a hunch, Rabbi Tokayer thought he would visit Japan's

Division of Foreign Cemeteries. Perhaps they would have the information he sought.

They gave him the names and addresses of two foreign cemeteries—the Inasa Foreign Cemetery and the Sakamoto Foreign Cemetery. On visits to both of these places, the chaplain failed to find any trace of a Jewish marker.

Almost ready to give up completely, Chaplain Tokayer decided to make one more trip to the Division of Foreign Cemeteries. Deep in the old files he found a tourist map, which indicated an out-of-the-way cemetery with a high wall around it. The map clearly marked the location of this cemetery.

Chaplain Tokayer stepped into a taxi and showed the driver the map with the location of this walled cemetery.

"If this isn't it," he said to himself as he rode out towards the cemetery, "then I give up. The Jewish cemetery must have been destroyed by the atom bomb."

As the chaplain stepped from the cab, he walked towards the gravestones. Inspecting the writing on the grave markers, he found Hebrew letters! The dates on the gravestones ranged from 1880 to 1920—exactly the date Mr. Gottlieb said the Jews left for Tokyo and Kobe. Finally, the chaplain had found the lost Jewish cemetery of Nagasaki!

Standing on top of the hill on which the cemetery is located, he could see how the hill crest protected the cemetery from the heat and blast of the atomic bomb. Still, it was many years since anyone had been there, and the graves were in deplorable condition.

Chaplain Tokayer mobilized all the resources in his power, and organized a task force of men to clean and restore the cemetery. Jewish military personnel stationed near Nagasaki along with men from the Jewish Community Center of Tokyo and the Israeli Embassy of Tokyo, joined hands on Lag B'Omer of 1964 and together restored the old cemetery. The chaplain chanted the memorial prayers. The men then got down on hands and knees, with buckets, brushes and soap and cleaned the grave markers. Others removed weeds, cleaned off the moss, and trimmed the grass.

After the ceremony of restoration was completed, the Israeli ambassador in Japan wrote to the Chief Rabbi of Israel who made an official record of the final resting-place of Nagasaki's one-time Jewish residents.

The rabbi in Tokyo assumed the responsibility of maintaining the cemetery and making sure that no one would ever have to repeat Chaplain Tokayer's efforts.

The Miraculous Seder in Saigon

CHAPLAIN DRYER'S UNEXPECTED PASSOVER IN VIETNAM

Chaplain Richard Dryer was sitting in his office at Fort Knox, Kentucky, in December, 1964, when he received news that the Jewish chaplain in Vietnam had just died. He would have to replace him, he was told, almost immediately.

By January 26, 1965, Chaplain Dryer was serving as the only rabbi in Vietnam. Since it takes so long for supplies to arrive in Vietnam, he thought he had better begin planning for the Passover Seder.

Some of the Jewish personnel in Saigon told him that it would be impossible to conduct a Seder in Saigon. There was so much fighting going on that war needs would not permit him the time or supplies to use for religious purposes on such short notice.

But he was determined to try.

Although his predecessor had ordered supplies of matza and wine from the Jewish Welfare Board, the number of troops stationed in Vietnam had doubled in one month, and more was needed.

Chaplain Dryer wrote to the Jewish Welfare Board which immediately contacted the Chief of Chaplains in Washington.

About ten days later, a cable arrived from Washington. "We are sending you 2500 pounds of matza and wine. You will also receive some through the U.S. Army Supply Services Command in Ryukyu Islands."

With this new information, the chaplain felt heartened. "With so much help, we will certainly have this Seder ready in time for Passover," he told his men. "Even Washington is fighting for us."

One of the high ranking Jews in Vietnam asked Rabbi Dryer where the Seder would be held.

"I don't know," said the chaplain. "Where would you suggest?"

"Actually," answered the Jewish colonel, "there is almost nowhere to have a celebration which could house so many people at once. We have no mess halls here like the ones in other military bases."

"What shall we do?" asked the chaplain.

The next day a phone call reached Chaplain Dryer from the Director of the USO, Mr. Gene Schram.

"I heard that you are looking for a place to conduct your Passover Seder, Chaplain," said Mr. Schram. "Why not use our USO facilities? Our snack bar staff would be more than happy to help you cook the meal and make preparations."

"What wonderful news!" answered the chaplain. "You have saved the holiday. I was almost ready to give up the whole idea."

Next came the problem of dishes. Again, the chaplain was stymied. Where could he possibly find place settings for 100 men which were not touched by leavened bread?

Once again, luck served the interests of the Jewish soldiers in Vietnam. The Navy Mess Section procured from Navy Supply Quartermaster enough brand new beautiful china for 100 men.

"With this kind of help," thought the chaplain to himself, "we are sure to be ready for the deadline date of April."

Only a short time later, an event occurred which almost cancelled the whole project of "Operation Passover Seder." News arrived on Friday afternoon that the Brink Hotel in Saigon had been bombed. Along with everything else and the many lives lost, all of the Navy's china dishes were smashed to bits.

But Chaplain Dryer did not let that stop him. He looked and looked until he arranged with the Army Supply System to borrow 100 plastic dishes, previously unused.

With a place to hold the Seder, dishes coming from the Army, wine and matza coming from the Chief of Chaplains in Washington through the Jewish Welfare Board, there were only a few things left to obtain. But these were essential: tables to eat on and extra stoves to handle the larger crowd expected on Passover Eve.

Chaplain Dryer wrote about his problem to the JWB. During a trip to Washington, the Director of the JWB's Commission on Jewish Chaplaincy happened to have an appointment with a State Department official, and he mentioned the problem of tables and stoves to him.

"That certainly does not sound like a great problem," said the official. "I'll see what I can do."

The next thing Chaplain Dryer knew, he was called by the U.S. Embassy in Saigon.

"When do you want the tables and stoves delivered, Chaplain?"

Chaplain Dryer again breathed a sigh of relief.

Now all of the facilities and material were ready, and the people could move into action.

Chaplain Dryer taught the Vietnamese snack bar manager,

Mr. Truong Binh Kien, how to cook for Passover, and he saw to it that not one crumb of *chometz* (leavened bread) came within a mile of the Passover food.

When the evening finally arrived, no one would have believed how beautiful it was. The Navy had lent their lovely white tablecloths, and the Marines a few men to serve as waiters.

The only Jewish woman in Saigon, a Navy librarian, lit the festival candles, and added the feminine touch to the scene. Only four months after sitting quietly in his office at Fort Knox, Kentucky, Chaplain Dryer was sitting in Saigon conducting the Passover Seder, something he never would have dreamed of doing in December. Through the efforts of the Chief of Chaplains, the JWB, the USO, the Army, Navy and Marines, Mr. Truong Binh Kien, a Navy librarian, and a host of other people, the first, nearly miraculous Seder was conducted in Saigon, Vietnam.

At the end of the Seder, the chaplain changed a few of the words of the Haggada. As the sound of gunfire and explosions were heard in the distance, Chaplain Richard Dryer rose from his seat and pronounced the ancient words, "This year we are here. May next year find us celebrating the Passover in Israel *or at home with our loved ones.*"